A Mind for Math
Level C

Genesis Curriculum
The Book of Genesis

First Edition

Welcome to *A Mind for Math*, the level C workbook. This workbook gives you a place for your daily work. You'll work through the lesson with your parent/teacher, listening and answering questions. You'll be doing each level of the lessons. This workbook will give you a place to write your answers and do your work.

It's good to learn to work the numbers in your head and use mental math, but it's also a good habit to write down work as well as the answers. Math will get more and more involved, and you won't always be able to do it in your head. Maybe on the first levels you can try to answer the questions in your head and just write down your answer, and then write the work out for the last level.

Most lessons are on one page, but sometimes it might go onto a second page.

Make sure to listen to the lessons and not just work ahead. In the lessons there will be more directions, more questions, and even hints for you.

Hope you have a great year. I hope that you'll find math fun and exciting.

Day 1

Add 12 hours for morning and 12 hours for evening together to see if you get one full day.

There was morning and evening, one day. If there had been morning, evening, and morning again, how long would that have been?

If there had been two full days, how long would that have been?

If there had been two "mornings" and two "evenings," how long would that have been?

Now add on another half a day.

Does 12 + 12 = 24?   Let's do that with two full days, 24 + 24.

What is forty plus eight?

Now, let's add two days and another half a day. How many hours do we need to add together?

Find the total number of hours in four days. That's the hours of two days plus the hours of two days.

Tens   Ones   Tens   Ones

Day 2

Which day comes after the second day?   Which day comes two before the fourth day?

Which day comes five after the third day?   Which day comes three before the tenth day?

Identify each number below as odd or even. (Write O or E under each.)

24   36   81   247   eighteenth   twelfth   fifteenth   100

Multiply five by:

14

17

19

26

Day 3

How many seeds did two apples produce if they produced 6 seeds? 7 seeds? 8 seeds? 9 seeds? 10 seeds?

Figure out how many seeds there would be if you had three apples and each had 1 seed. Then figure it out for 2 seeds, 3 seeds, 4 seeds, and 5 seeds. Skip count by threes.

What do you think happens when you quadruple or quintuple numbers? That's multiplying them by 4 or 5. Check to see if you are correct.

Is 123 x 256 an odd or even number?

Is 4,939 x 5,800 an odd or even number?

Multiply these numbers to check it out.

13 x 9

18 x 7

16 x 4

19 x 6

Day 4

Write one, ten, and one hundred on the chart below. Write two, twenty, and two hundred on the chart.

Hundreds Tens Ones

Write these numbers in the place value chart. 789   521   2,047   1,839
   Circle the greatest number.

Thousands Hundreds Tens Ones

Write these numbers in the place value chart. 5,421   20,647   18,309
   Circle the greatest number.

Ten Thousand Thousands Hundreds Tens Ones

Day 5
Review

How many hours are in three days?

Multiply these numbers by ten: 6, 7, 8.

Multiply five by 10, 11, 12, and 23.

Multiply.

    17 x 9   15 x 7

    16 x 8   19 x 4

Write these numbers in the place value chart. 2,724   13,457   18,096

Ten Thousand Thousands Hundreds Tens Ones

Day 6

Write in the answers to these multiplication questions.

5 x 2 =	5 x 3 =	5 x 4 =	5 x 5 =
5 x 6 =	5 x 7 =	5 x 8 =	4 x 0 =
4 x 1 =	4 x 2 =	4 x 3 =	4 x 4 =
4 x 5 =	4 x 6 =	4 x 7 =	4 x 8 =
5 x 6 =	4 x 7 =		3 x 9 =
8 x 8 =	7 x 6 =		9 x 5 =
10 x 3 =	11 x 4 =		12 x 6 =

13 x 8 =

14 x 7 =

15 x 9 =

Day 7

What is double one million?

Double these numbers: 7 8 9 10 100 400

Double these numbers: 14 32 50 241 430

     241
    +241

Double these numbers: 75, 98, 26, 48, 219. Add the hundreds. Add the tens. Add the ones. Put them all together.

     75

     98

     26

     48

     219

Day 8

Draw one line through each shape to divide it in half.

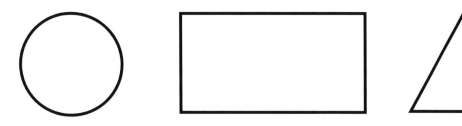

Draw another line on all those shapes to divide them in half another way.

Draw as many lines of symmetry as you can for a square.

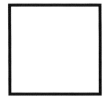

Shapes can have multiple, or many, lines of symmetry. How many lines of symmetry does the

triangle have?

the rectangle?

the circle?

Day 9

Count up objects in an area and as you count, make tally marks. Draw a line for each thing you count.

| | | | That shows you counted four things. When you get to five, you draw a line diagonally across the whole group.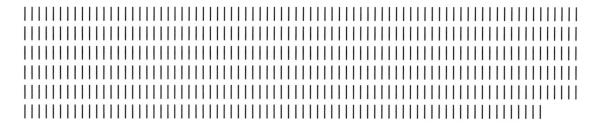

Count these lines with no tricks, just straight counting. Write down your answer.

Then use tally marks to bundle them into fives. Then you might want to divide them into groups of twenty or however else you find useful and then count them up.

Day 10
Review

Multiply.

5 x 7 =   6 x 6 =

9 x 6 =   9 x 3 =

10 x 8 =   11 x 6 =

12 x 7 =   14 x 8 =

Double these numbers: 35, 68, 16, 137. Add the hundreds. Add the tens. Add the ones. Put them all together.

Draw as many lines of symmetry as you can for this triangle where all the sides are the same length.

Make a shape with one line of symmetry. Fold a piece of paper in half and cut around the outside of the paper to make a design. Open up the paper. The fold is the line of symmetry.

Day 11

Double these numbers and read your answers out loud:

4   40   400   6   60   600   8   80   800

There are 140 plants and 70 are removed. How many are left?

Try it with these numbers and read your answers out loud:

$90 - 40$ $160 - 70$ $140 - 80$

$1100 - 300$ $800 + 900$

300 times 50 = 3 x 5 with three zeros = 15,000

Try this. How many pieces of fruit are in an orchard if there are 80 trees and each tree has 50 pieces of fruit?

Now try with these numbers and then read your answers out loud.

400 x 80

700 x 900

120 x 400

500 x 60

Day 12

```
tens ones
  4  | 1
  3  | 6
```

Now to expand numbers we break them up into tens and ones like this:

36 is 30 and 6. We write 30 + 6.

Expand 23, 56 and 81 in the same way. Turn them into addition problems that separate the tens and ones.

23   56   81

You can expand numbers with hundreds in the same way.

287 is 200 + 80 + 7 in expanded form, as we call it.

Expand.

517

628

349

Expand these numbers: 2571, 1080, 9804, and 6736. Write them in expanded form.

2571

1080

9804

6736

What is this number in standard form (just as a normal number)?   5000 + 700 + 20 + 3

Day 13

Draw a line. Pretend that's a river. Draw a line to divide it in half, split it in two. Here's the number one half. ½

If each side were a river, where could you draw two more lines to divide each of those rivers in half? Draw the lines. How many pieces of river do you have now?

Let's work with another shape. Draw a circle.

Divide the circle lake into four quarters by drawing a line to divide it in half and then another line to divide it in half the other way. Color in one half of the circle. How many fourths is that?

Draw one more circle and color in one quarter of it. When one quarter is colored in, how many fourths of that circle are not colored in?

Here is how you write one fourth. ¼   How do you write three fourths?

Draw another circle and pretend it's a lake. Color in one third of it. How many parts of the lake aren't colored in? How would you write that as a fraction?

Day 14

If there were 16 trees in the garden and the man were allowed to eat from them all except 8, how many trees was he allowed to eat from?

Now try with these numbers: 13 trees except 7, 14 trees except 5, 12 trees except 9

If there were 64 trees in the garden, and he were allowed to eat from all except 20, how many trees was he allowed to eat from?

Now try with these numbers: 55 trees except 13, 76 trees except 24, 90 trees except 40.

If there were 34 trees and he were allowed to eat from all of them except 25, how many trees was he allowed to eat from?

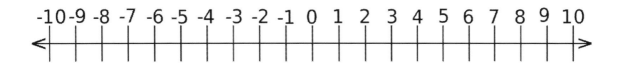

Try it with these numbers: 35 trees except 26, 41 trees except 35, 62 trees except 53

If he were allowed to eat from 82 trees except for 58 of them, how many were he allowed to eat from?

Now try it with these numbers: 93 trees except 38, 84 trees except 67, 75 trees except 49

Day 15
Review

How many pieces of fruit are in an orchard if there are 70 trees and each tree has 20 pieces of fruit?

Now try with these numbers. 280 x 30, 50 x 60

Expand these numbers: 8014 and 7610. Write them in expanded form.

What is this number in standard form (just as a normal number)?

8000 + 400 + 20 + 9

Draw a square. Color in one third of it and write the number one third.

If there were 54 trees and he were allowed to eat from all of them except 45, how many trees was he allowed to eat from?

Try it with these numbers: 43 trees except 25, 72 trees except 13.

Day 16

Adam had 24 ribs and God took away one. How many did he have left?

Practice subtraction by finding the differences between the number below and then make up a word problem about taking away for you parent to answer. You do it too so you can check if the answer is correct!

17	15	12	13	15	16
- 9	- 8	- 7	- 6	- 7	- 9

19	27	25	35	29	48
- 11	- 13	- 25	- 23	- 18	- 38

21	273	784	85	291
- 6	- 55	- 270	- 36	- 174

Day 17

Design a garden. Draw it out. Place your orchard. Draw a fence around it to keep out unwanted animals who would eat your fruit.

When you are done, measure around your garden. Measure each side to the nearest inch. A parent or older sibling can help you if you aren't sure how to measure. Write down the measurement of each side and then add them all together. That is the perimeter of your garden.

Then find the real measurement of your garden. Say that each inch is really 11 feet. How big is your garden?

> 1 inch on your drawing = 11 x 1 feet in real life

Day 18

There are patterns in today's reading. There's a pattern of behavior in Adam and Eve both blaming others for their sin. There's a pattern in God cursing each in turn, the serpent, the woman, and the man.

Today you are going to make patterns. A pattern is a repetition. You could repeat shapes, number, actions, rhythms.

An example of a shape pattern would be to draw a line, a circle, and a star, and then repeat it.

Everyone is going to make patterns for others to carry on. Find the pattern and continue it.

An example of a word pattern would be words that each start with the next letter of the alphabet: apple, bear, candle, dog, etc.

An example of a mathematical pattern would be to add five to each number like this: 1 6 11 16 21, etc.

Day 19

Look at this diagram. Picture the sword stationed at the letter B and it turning and putting its point at A, D, and C.

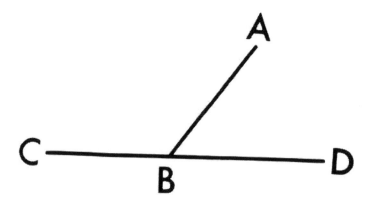

Draw 360 degrees on our ABCD picture.

Now what would be the measure of a half circle?

That would be the measure from where to where on our ABCD picture?

Lines have the angle measure of 180°. That's how we write degrees.

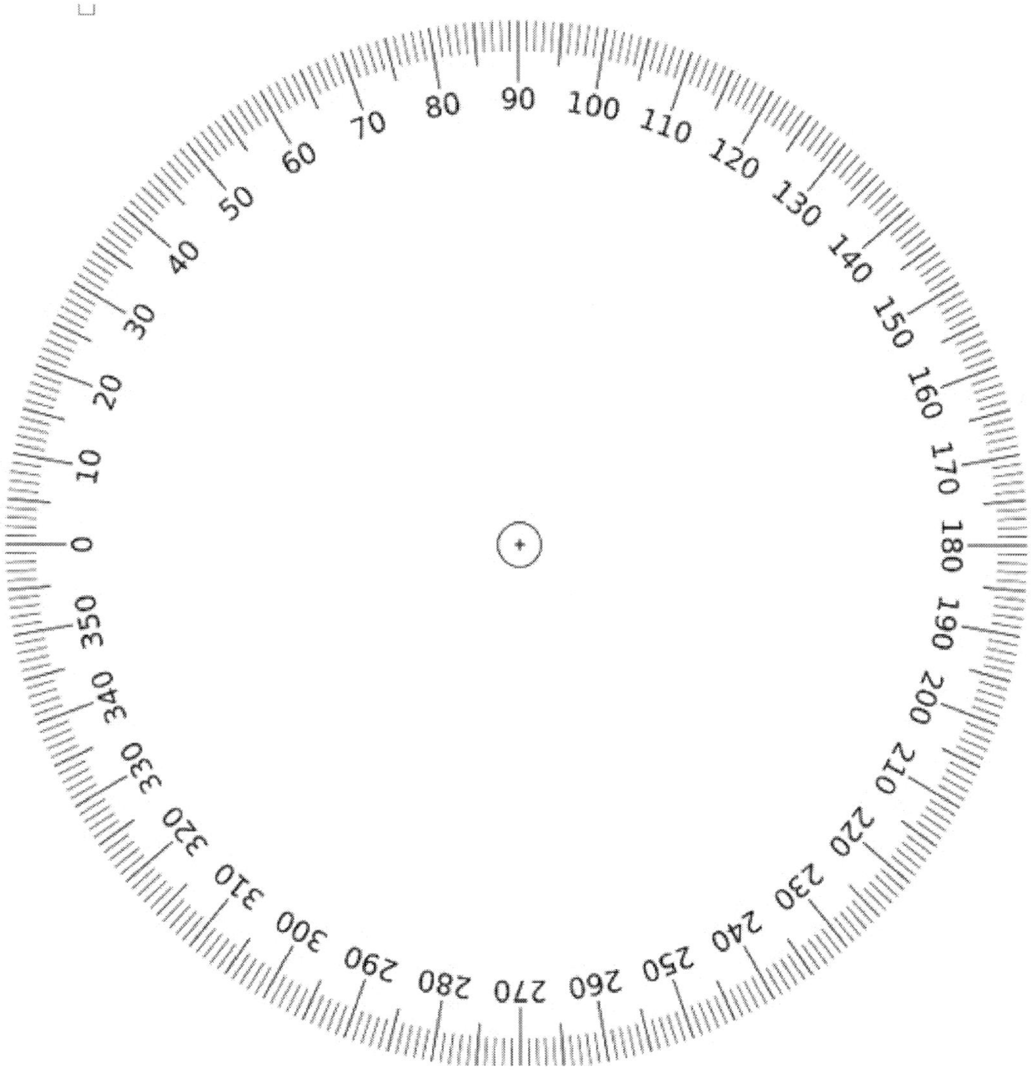
0
10
20
30
40
50
60
70
80
90
100
110
120
130
140
150
160
170
180
190
200
210
220
230
240
250
260
270
280
290
300
310
320
330
340
350

Day 20
Review

18	13	14	14	15	11
- 9	- 8	- 7	- 6	- 6	- 9

8	3	8	4	20	10
+ 9	+ 8	+ 7	+ 6	+ 20	+10

Find the perimeter of a book. Measure each side to the nearest inch and add them together. Count on for each side to find the total measure around.

What's the pattern in these numbers?

2, 4, 6, 8, 10, 12, 14, 16, 20

Draw a 360 degree angle.

Day 21

What hour would you read on these clocks?

What time does this clock say?

Read these clocks.

Day 22

Multiply 7 by 1, 2, 3, 5, and 10. Use skip counting. Use the chart to help you.

Multiplying is adding. Multiplying 1 x 7 = 1 + 1 + 1 + 1 + 1 + 1 +1. Add 2 + 2 + 2 + 2 + 2 + 2 + 2 and see if you get the same answer as when you multiplied and used skip counting.

Add fourteen to twenty-five. Write fourteen on the chart to show those answers.

tens	ones		tens	ones		tens	ones		tens	ones		tens	ones
2	5												

What if you were to add thirty-five to twenty-three or sixty-one to twenty-three?

What is 49, seven times? Do it by adding and then by multiplying.

What is 68, seven times? Do it by adding and then by multiplying.

Day 23

Draw four lines. Let's pretend Cain had four sons. If he built a city for half of them, how many had cities built for them? Circle half of the lines.

Redraw your four lines so that there are two together and then the other two together. Circle one in each pair.

If there were six sons and half of them had a city, how many had a city? Draw a picture to match your answer. Then write the fraction one half. It's the number one over the number two with a little line between them.

If a quarter of his sons had a city and he had eight sons, how many had cities? A quarter is one fourth, one out of every four. Draw a picture to show that. Find four and circle one of those. Then find another four.

Find one fourth of twelve sons and sixteen sons.

Can you find the pattern? If a quarter of his sons had a city and 5 sons had cities, how many sons did he have?

Find one third of 15 sons. Find two thirds of 21 sons. Label your answers.

Day 24

Put the symbol between the numbers below to show which is smaller and which is bigger.

23   51   102   78   124   160

Write which is the biggest.   17 + 14 or 28 + 5

Now try with these numbers.

1097   3012   230   200 + 15 + 17

What's greater 72 x 7 or 59 x 8?

Now try it with these numbers:

21,451   20,989   9 x 62   5 x 71

Day 25
Review

Read this clock.

What is 68, seven times? Do it by adding and then by multiplying.

Find one third of 18 sons. Find two thirds of 18 sons.

What's greater 38 x 7 or 42 x 8?

Compare these numbers.   13,451   9,999

Day 26
Review

176	483	508	452	91
+ 208	+ 125	+ 259	+ 263	+ 19

How many hours are in four days?

Multiply these numbers by ten: 5, 9.

Multiply six by 10, 11, 12, and 23.

What's greater?

48 x 4   27 x 8   10,001   9,999

Day 27
Review

196	274	351	158	567
+ 362	+ 180	+ 452	+ 27	+ 18

Multiply.

$8 \times 7 =$ $5 \times 6 =$

$9 \times 8 =$ $9 \times 4 =$

$10 \times 4 =$ $11 \times 8 =$

$12 \times 4 =$ $14 \times 9 =$

Double these numbers: 145, 263. Double the hundreds. Double the tens. Double the ones. Put them all together.

Find one third of 15 sons. Find two thirds of 15 sons.

Day 28
Review

$$1529 \qquad 3705 \qquad 2583 \qquad 569 \qquad 182$$
$$+\ \ 465 \qquad +\ 2738 \qquad +\ 6043 \qquad +\ 257 \qquad +\ 48$$

How many pieces of fruit are in an orchard if there are 180 trees and each tree has 30 pieces of fruit?

Write 7148 in expanded form.

What is 5000 + 20 + 6 in standard form (just as a normal number)?

What is 37, four times? Do it by adding and then by multiplying.

Day 29
Review

3008	1637	2158	560	427
+ 2835	+ 3329	+ 6534	+ 173	+ 289

Measure a book, each side to the nearest inch. Find the perimeter. Then find it if each inch really represented 7 feet.

Read this clock.

What's greater?

23 x 7   39 x 4

196	445	508	458	329
+ 202	+ 126	+ 254	+ 227	+ 195

240	287	254	165	473
+ 365	+ 283	+ 462	+ 378	+ 59

30	70	13	12	16
x 7	x 9	x 6	x 3	x 4

$70 + 70 + 70 + 70 + 70 + 70 =$

```
   21        273        754        355        246
-   6      -   90     - 270      -   81     - 174
```

346 + 257 =

17 x 3 =   16 x 9 =

19 x 3 =   15 x 5 =

Day 32
Review

```
  292        372        157        162        196
- 157      - 145      -  89      -  75      -  78
```

Multiply.

    27 x 8   36 x 7

Write this number in the place value chart. 38,126

<u>Ten Thousand Thousands Hundreds Tens Ones</u>

What's greater?

   13,451   12,897

Find one third of 12 sons. Find two thirds of 12 sons.

Day 33
Review

392	684	237	153	134
- 145	- 235	- 195	- 67	- 82

Draw a square. Draw on lines of symmetry. How many can you find?

Write the number one fourth.

If there were 82 trees and he were allowed to eat from all of them except 34, how many trees was he allowed to eat from?

Day 34
Review

217	375	158	463	564
- 9	- 49	- 79	- 78	- 182

Find the pattern in these numbers. What are the next two numbers?

50, 30, 40, 20, 30, 10

On the protractor draw a line from the center to the zero. Then draw a line to show 60 degrees.

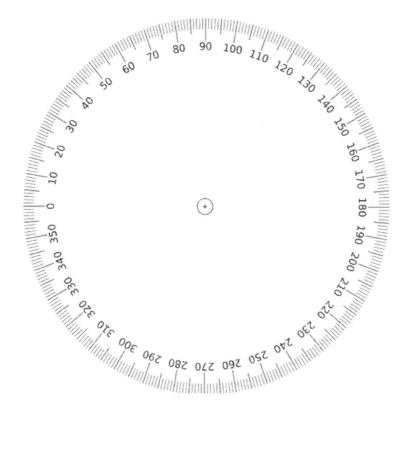

713	472	154	163	134
- 251	- 163	- 78	- 85	- 56

489	235	842	425	159
- 57	- 44	- 75	- 89	- 87

100 − 40 =

140 − 50 =

31 x 4 =   36 x 7 =

28 x 5 =   24 x 6 =

Day 36

$1 \times 2 = 2$ $2 \times 2 =$ $2 \times \quad =$ $2 \times \quad =$

Can you do it one more time?

Here's the first one $1 + 1 = 2$. Now keep going until you get to 64. Then how would you add 64 and 64?

Let's multiply by each of your previous answers: 2, 4, 8, 16, 32, 64, 128. Multiply them by 1, 2, 3, 4, 5, 6, and 7 respectively. (2×1, 4×2, 8×3, etc.)

Day 37

Figure out what goes in the blanks.

$8 +$ _____ $= 15$ $8 +$ _____ $= 14$ $8 +$ _____ $= 17$

$10 +$ _____ $= 15$ $20 +$ _____ $= 40$ $52 +$ _____ $= 75$

$45 +$ _____ $= 60$ $14 +$ _____ $= 22$ _____ $- 5 = 30$

Pay attention!

_____ $- 23 = 70$ 5 x _____ $= 75$

Think! Try!

$385 +$ _____ $= 392$ $154 +$ _____ $= 221$

Day 38

God gave Noah measurements for the ark: 300 cubits long, 50 cubits wide, 30 cubits high.

Find the perimeter in centimeters. Add up all the sides. How will you add 50 and 50? Look at how you can add 30 + 30.

$$\begin{array}{r} 30 \\ + 30 \\ \hline 0 \end{array} \qquad \begin{array}{r} 50 \\ + 50 \\ \hline \end{array} \qquad \begin{array}{r} 300 \\ + 300 \\ \hline \end{array}$$

Now, let's say that every 10 cubits is one inch. You would measure that by measuring 30 inches long and 5 inches wide. Measure that and mark it off.

Find the perimeter in inches.

Find the area for centimeters and inches, using the numbers above. Area is length times width. 10 x 10 is just 1 x 1 with two zeros tagged onto the end. 30 x 100 is 3 x 1 with two zeros tagged onto the end.

300 x 50 =

30 x 5 =

To find the volume of the boat, you multiply the length times the width times the height. Find the volume in inches and centimeters cubed.

Day 39

If seven of every clean animal entered the ark and two of every unclean animal, how many animals were there if there were three types clean animals and three types of unclean animals?

How many animals were there if there were just two types of the unclean and two types of the clean?

How many animals were there if there were five types of unclean animals and two types of clean animals?

Now figure out how many animals were on the ark if there were 5 types of each clean and unclean animals.

Try it with these numbers: 8 types of each, 4 types of each, 6 types of each.

Try it with these numbers: 12 types of each, 25 types of each, 37 types of each.

Day 40
Review

$$126 \times 8 =$$

Find what number fits in these blanks.

$$\_\_\_\_\_ - 23 = 70 \qquad 5 \times \_\_\_\_\_ = 75$$

$$385 + \_\_\_\_\_ = 392 \qquad 154 + \_\_\_\_\_ = 221$$

Find the area of a square with a length of 40 cm.

Now let's say it's a cube. What would the volume be?

Day 41

How many days does July, August, September, and October have all together?

How many minutes are in a day?

How many minutes are in a week?

Day 42

Let's say Noah sent out the dove at 10 AM and it stayed out until noon. How long was it gone? Draw each time on the clocks below and then write how much time has elapsed, how much time has gone by.

Elapsed time: Elapsed time: Elapsed time:

Now try with these times. Noon until 4 PM, 4 PM until 10 PM – For these, just draw the new time. You can use the previous clock to help you count the hours.

Let's say the dove flew past after half an hour but stayed out another two hours before it returned. How long did it stay out?

If Noah sent out the dove at 10:00, when did it return? Draw the time.

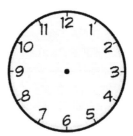

If the dove was sent out at ten in the morning and didn't return until three in the afternoon, how long was it out of the ark?

Draw these times on the clocks and then write how much time passed from the first to the second. 6:30 and 11:00

Elapsed Time:

Let's say Noah sent out the dove at 7:35 and it stayed out until 10:55. How long was the dove out of the ark? Draw the times and then figure out the elapsed time.

Elapsed time: Elapsed time:

Try again with these times. 11:50 and 12:05, 10:30 and 1:25, 4:15 and 9:40.

Elapsed time: Elapsed time:

Day 43

A penny is worth one cent.
A nickel is worth five cents.
A dime is worth ten cents.
A quarter is worth twenty-five cents.

$0.01 or 1¢ $0.05 or 5¢ $0.10 or 10¢ $0.25 or 25¢

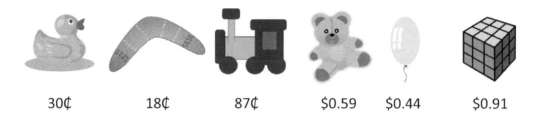

30¢   18¢   87¢ $0.59 $0.44 $0.91

Use your coins to buy the items. How many ways can you pay for each item?

How many ways can you make one dollar with coins? Write down at least ten different ways.

Add these amounts together. 30¢   18¢   87¢

How much would four trains cost?

Day 44

Count the worth of each group of coins and bills. One hundred and thirty cents is one dollar and thirty cents. We write it like this. $1.30

Now count your total starting with the highest bill. How much money do you have?

Add the amounts from part A and see if you get the amount in part B.

$1.99
+ $2.99
$4.98

Then double the amount. And again! And again?

Day 45
Review

How many minutes are in two days?

Let's say Noah sent out the dove at 5:25AM and it stayed out until 9:45PM. How long was the dove out of the ark? Draw the times and then figure out the elapsed time.

Elapsed time: 11:20AM to 4:15PM
                                           Elapsed time:

Add these amounts together. 62¢   53¢   74¢

How much would four trains cost if they were each $1.87?

How much would seven trains cost?

Day 46

If the Tower of Babel were 45 feet tall, and the next tallest building was 23 feet tall, how much taller was the Tower of Babel?

If the Tower of Babel were 57 feet tall, and the next tallest building was 45 feet tall, how much taller was the Tower of Babel?

If the Tower of Babel were twelve feet taller than the previous tallest building which was twenty-five feet tall, then how tall was the Tower of Babel?

If the Tower of Babel were forty-one feet taller than the previous tallest building which was eighteen feet tall, then how tall was the Tower of Babel?

If the Tower of Babel were 425 feet tall, and the next tallest building was 210 feet tall, how much taller was the Tower of Babel?

If the Tower of Babel were 657 feet tall, and the next tallest building was 452 feet tall, how much taller was the Tower of Babel?

If the Tower of Babel were twenty-four meters taller than the previous tallest building which was seventeen meters tall, then how tall was the Tower of Babel?

If the Tower of Babel were forty-nine meters taller than the previous tallest building which was eighteen meters tall, then how tall was the Tower of Babel?

If the Tower of Babel were 52 yards tall, and the next tallest building was 13 yards tall, how much taller was the Tower of Babel?

If the Tower of Babel were 75 yards tall, and the next tallest building was 58 yards tall, how much taller was the Tower of Babel?

If the Tower of Babel were twenty-seven hundred inches (2700 ft) taller than the previous tallest building which was fifteen thousand inches tall, then how tall was the Tower of Babel?

If the Tower of Babel were four times taller than the previous tallest building which was eighty-six feet tall, then how tall was the Tower of Babel?

Day 47

If it were 5 miles from Ur to Shechem and 12 miles from
Shechem to the Negev, how far did Abraham travel all together?

If it were 52 kilometers from Ur to Shechem and 27 miles from
Shechem to the Negev, how far did Abraham travel all together?

If the trip was 18 miles and the first part was 7 miles,
how long was the second part of the trip?

If the trip was 78 kilometers and the first part was
43 kilometers, how long was the second part of the trip?

If it were 55 miles from Ur to Shechem and 19 miles from
Shechem to the Negev, how far did Abraham travel all together?

If it were 247 kilometers from Ur to Shechem and 37 miles from
Shechem to the Negev, how far did Abraham travel all together?

If the trip was 180 miles and the first part was 90 miles,
how long was the second part of the trip?

If the trip was 385 kilometers and the first part was
143 kilometers, how long was the second part of the trip?

If it were 512 miles from Ur to Shechem and 128 miles from
Shechem to the Negev, how far did Abraham travel all together?

If it were 328 kilometers from Ur to Shechem and 380 miles
from Shechem to the Negev, how far did Abraham travel all together?

If the trip was 180 miles and the first part was 77 miles,
how long was the second part of the trip?

If the trip was 758 kilometers and the first part was
429 kilometers, how long was the second part of the trip?

Day 48

Abraham is on a journey. Draw a line that is one inch long. Draw a line that is three centimeters long. Which is longer?

Now draw Abraham's journey. Use the ruler. How long did you draw your line?

Draw a line that's three and a half inches long. Then draw one that is six and a half centimeters long. Which is longer?

Now draw Abraham's journey. How long did you draw your line?

Draw five lines or measure five small things in your house and write down their measurement in centimeters. There are ten lines for each centimeter. We can write tenths like this.

0.1 one tenth, 0.2 two tenths, 0.3 three tenths, etc. Each line is one tenth. Just count them up. If it measured seven centimeters and then eight more little lines, the answer would be 7.8.

Day 49

10   11   12   13   14   15   16   17   18   19   20

Round to the nearest ten.

31 →   58 →   42 →   17 →

When a number ends in a 5, it's right in the middle of the number line. We just make the decision to always round it up. So 25 rounds up to 30, 35 rounds up to 40, 45 rounds up to 50, etc.

13 →   35 →   46→   65→

100   110   120   130   140   150   160   170   180   190   200

Round the numbers below to the nearest hundred.

143 →   450 →   129→   680→

Day 50
Review

If the Tower of Babel were 64 yards tall, and the next tallest building was 28 yards tall, how much taller was the Tower of Babel?

If the Tower of Babel were seven times taller than the previous tallest building which was forty-five feet tall, then how tall was the Tower of Babel?

If it were 285 kilometers from Ur to Shechem and 473 kilometers from Shechem to the Negev, how far did Abraham travel all together?

If the trip was 528 kilometers and the first part was 295 kilometers, how long was the second part of the trip?

Draw three lines or measure three small things in your house and write down their measurement in centimeters.

100   110   120   130   140   150   160   170   180   190   200

Round the numbers below to the nearest hundred.

139 →   357 →   125 →   661 →

Day 51

- 144   can of Coke
- 108   homemade biscuit
- 68   slice of bread
- 240   package of M&Ms
- 110   Cheerios (1 ¼ cups)
- 51   homemade chocolate chip cookies
- 140   goldfish, 45 crackers
- 377   one cup of soft vanilla ice cream
- 188   one slice of cheese pizza, Dominos
- 111   one scrambled egg with butter and milk
- 80   apple
- 71   orange
- 117   one cup of apple juice
- 406   extra-crispy chicken thigh from KFC
- 520   quarter-pounder with cheese from McDonald's
- 288   4 ounces of lean ground beef
- 190   a serving of salted peanuts

Let's say that you ate a homemade biscuit, an apple, and a scrambled egg. How many calories did you consume?

How many calories did you eat if you had an orange and Cheerios for breakfast?

If you had two chocolate chip cookies, how many calories did you eat?

How many calories did you consume if you at a quarter-pounder with cheese from McDonald's and an extra-cripsy chicken thigh from KFC and a chocolate chip cookie?

Plan out breakfast, lunch, and dinner. Choose at least three foods "to eat" for each meal. Then figure out the calorie total of each meal.

Total your calories for the day.

If you ate that every day for seven days, how many calories would you have consumed?

Now figure it out for 4 and 9 days.

Read your answers out loud.

Day 52

If a man was sixty-eight years old, how long ago was he three years old?

How old he was fifty-seven years from the time he was three.

If the man was forty-nine years old, how long ago was he three?

If an animal was 47 months old, how old would she be in 8 months?

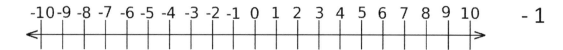
- 1

Let's say we're trying to get to 50. We have 31. Subtract 31 from 50 to see how much more we need.

Try it with these numbers: 50 – 12, 50 – 24, 20 - 8

If twenty-seven animals were all eight years old, how many years total had they all been alive?

What if there had been seventy-six of them?

If a man was one hundred three years old, how old was he eighteen years ago?

If the man was one hundred ten years old, how old was he thirty-eight years ago?

Day 53

If Abraham had lived in Canaan from January 3rd to January 27th, how long had he lived there?

If Abraham lived in Canaan from January 3rd until the end of the month, how long did he live there?

Now how many days did he live there, if he lived there all of January and until February 15th?

How many days did he live there if he was in Canaan during all of March, April, May, and June?

How many days did Abraham live in Canaan if he lived there just during the months of January, March, June, and December?

If Abraham lived in Canaan from January first through the end of March, how many days did he stay? (no leap year)

If he ended up staying 21 days less than that, how long did he live there?

If Abraham lived there for thirty-four weeks, how many days did he stay?

If Abraham lived there for forty-six weeks, how many days did he stay?

If Abraham lived there for forty-three days less than one hundred days, how many days did he stay?

If Abraham lived there for thirty-two days less than one hundred fourteen days, how many days did he stay?

Day 54

Multiply.

10 x 5 =   20 x 5 =

15 x 10 =   25 x 8 =

124 x 3 =

426 x 9 =

278 x 7 =

379 x 6 =

Day 55

Review

Calories

406	extra-crispy chicken thigh
188	one slice of cheese pizza
111	one scrambled egg with butter and milk

Total your calories for the day if you add the foods above.

If you ate that every day for seven days, how many calories would you have consumed?

If forty-five animals were all eight years old, how many years total had they all been alive?

What if there had been eighty-seven of them?

If a man was one hundred and five years old, how old was he nineteen years ago?

If lived there twenty-nine days less than seventy-one weeks, how many days did he stay?

If Abraham lived there for sixty-four days less than one hundred days, how many days did he stay?

Multiply.   714 x 5 =   289 x 3 =

Day 56

90   91   92   93   94   95   96   97   98   99   100

If Sarah were 93 and Abraham 99, <u>about</u> how old is that added together?

Try it with these numbers. Estimate the answers.

42 + 48 =   51 + 59 =

27 + 31 =   94 + 91 =

Estimate. About how much is 78 + 63?

Now try with these numbers: 44 + 75, 15 + 57, 39 + 26

Estimate. About how much is 159 - 76? (Pay attention.)

Now try with these numbers: 170 - 29, 114 - 68, 155 - 82.

Day 57

Draw 6:30, three thirty, and half past ten.

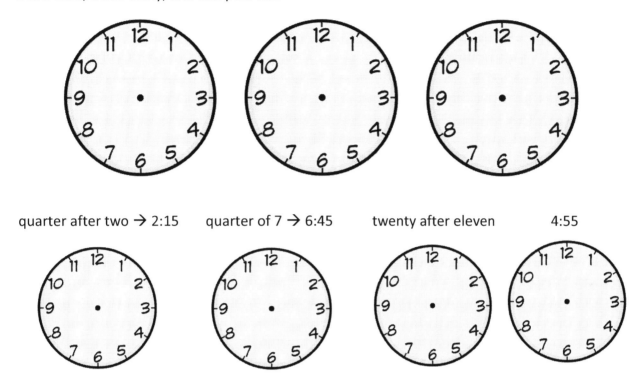

quarter after two → 2:15   quarter of 7 → 6:45   twenty after eleven   4:55

Draw 7:17 on the second clock below. How much time elapses from 3:34 to 7:42 if both times are PM on the same day?

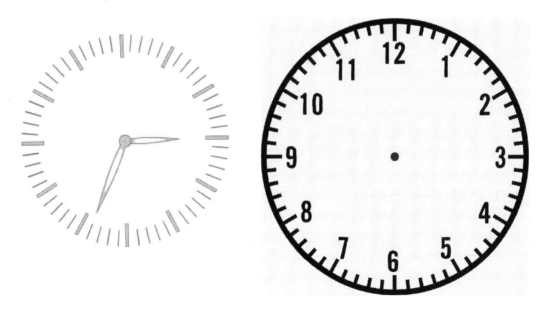

Day 58

hundreds	tens	ones
1	0	0
+	9	0
1	9	0

Add together. Make sure to add together the correct place values.

200 + 500 =   40 + 50 =   210 + 6 =   105 + 3 =

tens	ones
10	0
9	0

hundreds	tens	ones
1	0	0
	10	0
		100

Subtract:

140 − 70 =   120 − 80 =   150 − 90 =   110 − 30 =

Subtract 142 − 85. Here are two ways to look at it. What did I do in each example?

```
   142
 -  85
    60
  -  3
    57
```

hundreds	tens	ones
	13	12
	- 8	5
	5	7

Subtract and find the difference.

240 − 152 =   424 − 185 =

326 − 97 =   126 − 89 =

Day 59

Let's do righteous/unrighteous fractions. Draw a square and draw a line to divide it in half. Color in one half. We write fractions like this:

$\frac{1}{2}$ or when typing I write them like this ½ or like this $^1/_2$

Draw a line through the middle of those rectangles from side to side. Color in one more box. How many of the four boxes are colored in?

If there were two people and one was righteous, how could you write as a fraction how many of the people were righteous?

How would you write the fraction that would show how many were unrighteous?

Write the fraction that would show the number of unrighteous people if there were four people all together and only one was unrighteous.

Write the fraction that would show the number of righteous if there were three people and only one was righteous.

Write the fraction that would show the number of unrighteous in that scenario.

Let's say that there was a group of eight people. Let's say that five were righteous. Write the number of righteous and the number of unrighteous as fractions. Then use the > greater than sign or the < less than sign to show which fraction is greater (which animal has more

Do it again with a group of 13 all together and 7 are unrighteous.

Day 60
Review

Estimate.

172 – 34 =   111 – 72 =   157 – 75 =

Draw 3:24 and 6:47. How much time passes between them?

Subtract and find the difference.

150 – 123 =   327 – 136 =

264 – 175 =   165 – 97 =

Draw a picture that shows four out of five. Write the fraction to match the color.

Day 61

236 x 5 =

Find what number fits in these blanks.

_____ - 39 = 48   257 + _____ = 392

Find the area of a square with a length of 50 cm.

Now let's say it's a cube. What would its volume be?

Day 62

```
  123          100          241          100
   45         - 40          294         - 37
+ 315                     + 318
```

How many minutes are in three days?

Let's say Noah sent out the dove at 8:15AM and it stayed out until 7:35PM. How long was the dove out of the ark? Draw the times and then figure out the elapsed time.

Elapsed time:

Add these amounts together.   26¢   35¢   47¢

How much would four trains cost if they were each $2.73?

Day 63 (ruler)

```
   823        1100        241        100
    95       - 400       x  5       - 58
 + 325
```

If the Tower of Babel were 82 yards tall, and the next tallest building was 34 yards tall, how much taller was the Tower of Babel?

If it were 254 kilometers from Ur to Shechem and 381 miles from Shechem to the Negev, how far did Abraham travel all together?

Draw a line that is five and a half centimeters long.

```
100   110   120   130   140   150   160   170   180   190   200
```

Round the numbers below to the nearest hundred.

125 →   375 →   80 →   710→

Day 64

```
  517        100         48        100
   73        -  4         94        - 62
+ 248                   + 263
```

Calories
188   one slice of cheese pizza

If you had four slices of cheese pizza, how many calories would you have consumed?

If seventy-two animals were all eight years old, how many years total had they all been alive?

If a man was one hundred and five years old, how old was he thirty-six years ago?

If lived there twenty-eight days less than sixty-five weeks, how many days did he stay?

Day 65

```
  513          500          192          500
   75        -  80          704        -  29
+ 969                     + 248
```

```
  823         1100          241          100
   95        -  400          175        -  58
+ 325                      + 430
```

```
  317          145          289
x   5        x   6        x   4
```

Day 66

```
   586          $1.00          185          $1.00
 + 75         - $0.30        + 378        - $0.48
```

Estimate.

168 – 25   105 - 74

Draw 2:36 and 7:52. How much time passes between them.

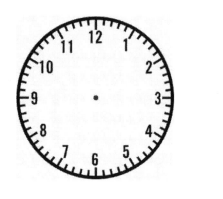 

Subtract and find the difference.

520 – 232

Day 67

```
   486        $1.00        964        $1.00
 + 187      - $0.80      +  87      - $0.36
```

$234 \times 7 =$

Draw a picture that shows three out of seven. Write the fraction to match.

Find what number fits in these blanks.

_____ - 13 = 63   527 + _____ = 680

Find the area of a square with a length of 70 cm.

Day 68

600	$11.00	138	$1.00
85	- $4.00	x 7	- $0.71
+ 315			

Let's say Noah sent out the dove at 8:15AM and it stayed out until 5:55PM. How long was the dove out of the ark? Draw the times and then figure out the elapsed time.

Elapsed time:

Add these amounts together. 52¢   39¢   84¢

How much would it cost to buy seven trains if one cost $3.45?

Day 69

How much would four trains cost if one train was 93 cents?

723	$1.00	47	$1.00
97	- $0.60	x 6	- $0.38
+ 255			

If the Tower of Babel were 164 yards tall, and the next tallest building was 82 yards tall, how much taller was the Tower of Babel?

If it were 253 kilometers from Ur to Shechem and 147 kilometers miles from Shechem to the Negev, how far did Abraham travel all together?

100   110   120   130   140   150   160   170   180   190   200

Round the numbers below to the nearest hundred.

99 →   350 →   105 →   741 →

Day 70

```
   271        1500         97        $1.00
    48       - 800        607      - $0.29
 + 469                  + 322
```

```
   123        1400        441        $1.00
    58       - 500        105      - $0.17
 + 194                  + 538
```

```
   428         256         380
 x   5       x   6       x   4
```

Day 71

Write the fraction one half.

Write one third, draw one out of three parts, and draw one of three things.

Now write two thirds and draw pictures to show two thirds.

Write three fourths and draw pictures to show that fraction?

How much is one third plus one third?

Write the equation and answer and draw a picture to show it.

Now add one quarter and three quarters and draw pictures. What's the answer?

Day 72

Draw a picture and write a fraction that shows each of the following fractions: one half, one third, one fourth, one fifth, one sixth.

Can you draw a picture to show one and one half? How do you think you write one and one half?

Write three and two thirds, four and five sixths, and twelve and three sevenths.

Find the sum or difference.　Examples:　$3\frac{1}{2} + 2\frac{1}{2} = 5\frac{2}{2} = 5$ and $1 = 6$

$1\frac{1}{4} - \frac{3}{4} = (\frac{4}{4}$ and $\frac{1}{4}) - \frac{3}{4} = \frac{5}{4} - \frac{3}{4} = \frac{2}{4} = \frac{1}{2}$

$\frac{2}{6} + \frac{4}{6} =$　　　　　　　　　$\frac{1}{5} + \frac{2}{5} =$

$\frac{2}{3} - \frac{1}{3} =$　　　　　　　　　$\frac{4}{6} - \frac{3}{6} =$

$23\frac{2}{6} + 24\frac{3}{6} =$　　　　　　　$18\frac{3}{7} + 5\frac{1}{7} =$

$4\frac{4}{6} - 1\frac{3}{6} =$　　　　　　　　$14\frac{5}{6} - 7\frac{1}{6} =$

Day 73

Draw ten circles. Color in one of them. How do you think you would write the fraction to show that number?

Color in one more and write a fraction to show that number. Then keep doing it until all the circles are colored in.

A tenth can be written as a decimal as well. It looks like this.   0.1

How do you think you would write two tenths?

Write each tenth fraction as a decimal.

0.1 is the same as 0.10. That's the same as $0.10. That's the same as ten cents. How much is ten dimes?

Write addition and subtraction equations as either fractions or decimals. Answer all of them. Here are examples. To add decimals. We add just like regular numbers but make sure the decimal point stays in the same place.

.2 + .5 = $\frac{4}{10} + \frac{5}{10} =$

.1 + .5 = $\frac{2}{10} + \frac{6}{10} =$

.4 - .3 = $\frac{8}{10} - \frac{7}{10} =$

Day 74

You can write one tenth as a decimal as well.   0.1

How would you write two tenths?

0.1 is the same as 0.10. That's the same as $0.10. That's the same as ten cents. How do you think you would write twenty cents?

Write thirty, forty, fifty, sixty, seventy, eighty, ninety, and one hundred cents.

Now let's add those together. Start with ten cents plus twenty cents. $0.10
                                                                                                    + $0.20

Keep going. Add on thirty cents then forty cents...

Multiply those answers by 7.

Day 75
Review

$2/7 + 4/7 =$ $1/9 + 4/9 =$

$3/8 + 4/8 =$ $3\,2/3 - 1\,1/3 =$

$14\,3/5 - 8\,1/5 =$ $30\,7/9 - 16\,2/9 =$

Write one tenth through ten tenths as money amounts and then multiply each one by eight and then add all the answers together.

Day 76

If we had 100 books at home and gave 50 to the library for their book sale, how many books are still at home?

```
  100
-  50
   50
```

Find the difference using these numbers.

$150 - 80 =$ $\qquad$ $160 - 90 =$ $\qquad$ $130 - 60 =$ $\qquad$ $120 - 40 =$

If you had 123 books at home and took fifty to the library, how many books did you still have at home?

If you had 123 books at home and took 55 to the library, how many books did you still have at home?

Find the difference using these numbers.

$123 - 64$, $145 - 58$, $127 - 39$, $114 - 37$

Day 77

This is how you write ten cents. 10 ¢ or $0.10

This is how you write five cents and one cent. 5 ¢ or $0.05   1 ¢ or $0.01

What are these coins? What are their names and how much are they worth? Write the amount they are worth using a dollar sign.

Count up the value of these coins. Write the amount with a dollar sign.

Write down five cents plus five cents equals ten cents in a different way.
     5 ¢ + 5 ¢ = 10 ¢

Combine coins that equal a dollar into two piles. Write down at least two equations. Use a dollar sign. Example: $0.50 + $0.50 = $1.00

Then write two subtraction equations using what you just wrote.
Example: $1.00 - $0.50 = $0.50

To subtract from one dollar, you need to be able to subtract from 100. Do you see the similarity?
100 and $1.00

$2.13
+ $1.49
$.

What's 100 – 40? Look at the example below. It's just like subtracting 10 – 4. Can you see it?

100
- 40

What's $1.00 - $0.40?

What's $1.00 - $0.43?

Subtract. Then check to see if your answers make sense! Add the answer and what you subtracted together, even use coins to do it. Do they make a dollar?

$1.00 $1.00 $1.00 $1.00 $1.00
-$0.30   -$0.53   -$0.78   -$0.16   -$0.24

Day 78

If Isaac was born at 6 AM and eight days later was circumcised at noon, how old was he to the hour, eight days and how many hours?

How many hours are there from 8 AM until 4 PM?

Draw two times and write how much time passes between them.

Elapsed time:

If he had been born at 12:30 AM and was circumcised at noon eight days later, how old was he to the minute?

How many minutes pass from 12:15 PM until 1:00 PM? How long is it from 5:15 AM until 3:30 PM?

How long is it from 8:45 AM until 1:30 PM? Draw two times and write how much time passes between them.

Elapsed time:

Eight days passed. How many hours is that?

How many minutes is that?

If it had been eighteen days, how many hours would that have been?

Day 79

If Isaac got one half of the inheritance from Abraham, how much would Ishmael get?

If Isaac got one third of the inheritance, how much would Ishmael get if he got the rest?

If Isaac got one fourth of the inheritance, how much would Ishmael get if he got the rest?

If Ishmael and Isaac each got one half of ten dollars, how much would they each get?

If they each got half of one hundred dollars, how much would they get?

If they each got half of one thousand dollars, how much would they get?

If they each got half of one dollar, how much would they get?

If they each got half of 50 cents, how much would they each get?

If they each got half of 50 dollars, how much would they each get?

If they each got half of 500 dollars, how much would they each get?

Find half of these numbers by multiplying by .5, which to do that you just multiply by 5 and then add a decimal place to your answer.

63, 153, 4931, 784

Day 80
Review

Find the difference.

234 – 75, 351 – 87

Subtract. Then check to see if your answers make sense! Add the answer and what you subtracted together, even use coins to do it. Do they make a dollar?

$$\begin{array}{r} \$1.00 \\ -\$0.40 \\ \hline \end{array} \qquad \begin{array}{r} \$1.00 \\ -\$0.37 \\ \hline \end{array} \qquad \begin{array}{r} \$1.00 \\ -\$0.84 \\ \hline \end{array}$$

Multiply. 46 x 27 and 38 x 45.

Multiply these numbers by 0.50 and 0.30.

75, 392

Day 81

Let's look at the lay of the land. Let's look at shapes. I'm going to show you shapes, and you tell me what they are and how you know.

Identify the three-dimensional shapes and tell how you know what shape it is. Describe it.

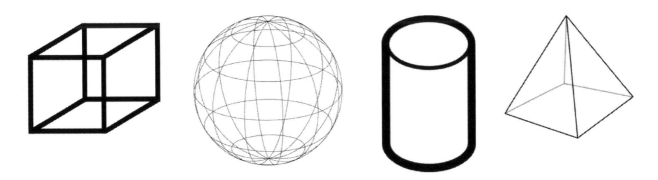

What's a congruent shape? Identify the shapes and describe how to identify that shape. They are all polygons. A polygon is a flat, closed figure with straight sides.

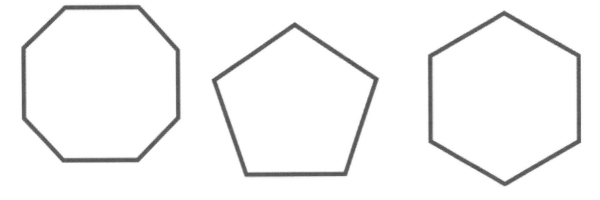

Day 82

```
 35      14        26      39
- 21    + 21      + 13    - 13
 14      35 ✓      39      26 ✓
```

Answer these questions and then check your work.

```
   56            12            74
 - 14          + 35          - 43
```

```
   50           217           272            79
 - 34          + 75          - 156          + 47
```

Do the opposite to check my work.

225 ÷ 15 = 15   2788 ÷ 34 = 81   735 ÷ 5 = 149   2104 ÷ 8 = 263

Day 83

We're going to convert fractions into decimals. Follow the pattern to convert the fractions into decimals.

$1/10$ $2/10$ $3/10$ $4/10$ $5/10$

0.1   0.2   0.3   0.4

$6/10$ $7/10$ $8/10$ $9/10$

Do the opposite. Convert the decimals into fractions.

0.1   0.2   0.3   0.4   0.5   0.6   0.7   0.8   0.9

Write these numbers as decimals and then convert them to mixed numbers: seven and one tenth, eight and seven tenths, twelve and nine tenths, five and five tenths.

Compare the first two and the last two numbers (that you just wrote). Draw a greater than and less than symbol between them.

What else does five out of ten equal? How else could you write five tenths and have it mean the same amount?

Day 84

The first rectangle is all the wood together in its bundle. That represents how big it is. Divide the next rectangle in half. Color in one half of it. Divide the next rectangle by four. Color in one quarter. Divide the last rectangle by three. Draw two lines to make three parts. Color in one third.

Use the greater than/less than symbol to show which is biggest in each pair.

We write one half like this. $^1/_2$ We write two halves like this. $^2/_2$ $^2/_2 = 1$ $^{100}/_{100} = 1$

How many quarters do you need to make a half? How do you write 2 out of 4 parts as a fraction?

How many quarters do you need to make a whole?

How do you write 4 out of 4 parts as a fraction? What whole number does $^4/_4$ equal?

What's bigger: three fourths or one? Write your answer using < or >.

Write an addition and a subtraction equation that give the answer $^3/_4$.

Now write an addition equation and a subtraction equation with the answer $^3/_8$.

½ x 10   or   ½ (10)   or   ½ * 10   These are a half of ten. Write an equation that would give you a quarter of sixteen.

Day 85
Review

Which of these is a polygon?

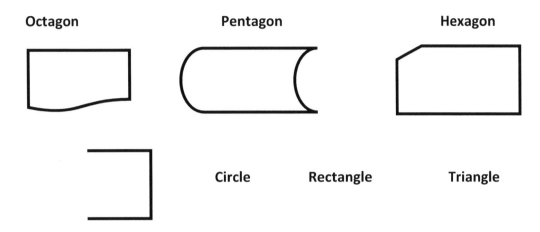

Octagon   Pentagon   Hexagon

Circle   Rectangle   Triangle

Do the opposite to check my work.

2314 ÷ 9 = 247

Write three tenths and one tenth as fractions and decimals.

Convert the decimals into fractions or the fractions into decimals.

0.1   0.2   0.3   0.4   0.5

6/10   7/10   8/10   9/10

Write an addition equation and a subtraction equation that give the answer 5/7.

Day 86

A car weighs at least two tons. A baby weighs about 8 pounds. A slice of bread weighs almost one ounce. How would you weigh a heavy stone in tons, pounds, or ounces?

What measure would you use to weigh a handful of nuts? What measure would you use to weigh a mobile home? What would you use to weigh a book? What about a big box of books?

A bag of potatoes weighing a kilogram has about seven potatoes inside. A slice of bread is about 29 grams. Which estimate is best for these items?

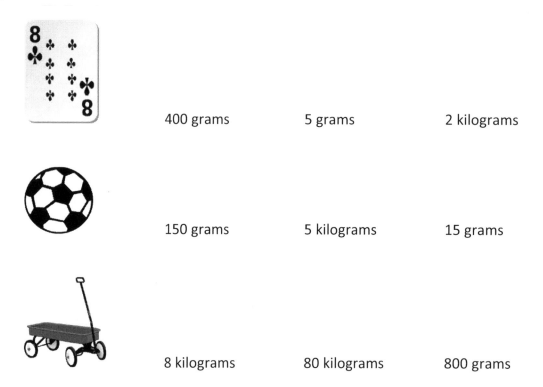

400 grams	5 grams	2 kilograms
150 grams	5 kilograms	15 grams
8 kilograms	80 kilograms	800 grams

A gram is one thousandth of a kilogram. A kilogram is one thousand grams. Write these measures as the other.

2000 grams   4 kilograms

500 grams   1.5 kilograms

Day 87

If the altar weighed nine hundred pounds and eight hundred pounds of ram were on top of the altar, how much would the whole thing weigh?

If the altar weighed 8 ounces without the ram and the ram weighed 5 ounces, how much would it weigh all together?

What if the whole thing all together weighed 16 pounds and the ram weighed 8 pounds, how much did the altar weigh without the ram on top?

If all together the ram and altar weighed 14 kilograms and the ram weighed 5 kilograms, how much did the altar weigh without the ram?

If the altar weighed 153 tons and 25 tons of ram was on top, how much did it all weigh together?

If all together it weighed 351 grams, how much did the ram weigh if the altar alone weighed 327 grams?

If the altar weighed 209 ounces and the ram weighed 57 ounces, how much did the altar weigh after the ram was placed on it?

If the altar weighed eight times as much as the ram on it and the ram was 73 tons, how much did the altar weigh?

If the altar weighed five times as much as the ram at 67 ounces, how much did it weigh?

If the altar weighed forty-seven times the weight of the ram on it, how much did it weigh if the ram is fifteen ounces.

If the altar weighs 64 times the weight of the ram on it, and the ram is 320 grams, how much does the altar weigh?

Day 88

Draw a line on the page. Then use a ruler to measure it to the nearest inch.

Then draw lines that are three inches long, five inches long, and seven inches long.

Add together your measurements.

Draw lines that are two centimeters, four centimeters, and eight centimeters long. Are those numbers all odd or even?

Add together those measurements.

Now measure the first line you drew to the nearest half inch.

Draw lines that are 3.5 inches long, 2.5 inches long, 1.5 inches long.

Add together those measurements.

Day 89

If we bought the toy for five dollars and sold the toy for eight dollars, how much profit did we make? This is how you write that with a dollar sign. **$3.00**

Figure out your profit. Buy at $4.00 and sell at $8.00.

Buy at twelve dollars and sell at twenty-six dollars.

Buy at twenty-one cents and sell at forty-five cents.

Buy at $0.35 and sell at $0.79.

Buy at $6.35, and sell at $10.50.

Buy at $24.23, and sell at $37.45.

Buy at $112.03, and sell at $150.22.

Buy at $46.18, and sell at $61.25.

What happens when you have negative cents after you subtract? Look at this example. Buy at $1.20, and sell at $3.15. These are all the same.

$3.15	315	315	315	315
- $1.20	- 120	-120	-120	-120
2.00	200	205	200	205
-.10	-10	- 10	190	195
+.05	5	195	195	
$1.95	195			

Find your profit. Buy at $15.02, and sell at $23.15.

Buy at $13.67, and sell at $46.19.

Buy at $53.69, and sell at $80.50.

Buy at $23.85, and sell at $30.80.

Day 90
Review

Find your profit. Buy at $15.32, and sell at $64.15. Buy at $27.65, and sell at $48.29.

If the altar weighed seven times as much as the ram on it and the ram was 143 pounds, how much did the altar weigh?

If the altar weighs thirty-eight times the weight of the ram on it, how much does the altar weigh if the ram is twenty-five pounds.

If the altar weighs 49 times the weight of the ram on it, and the ram is 260 ounces, how much does the altar weigh?

What's 4500 grams in kilograms?

What's 1.2 kilograms in grams?

Draw a line that is 2.5 inches long.

Day 91

We don't know how many people were there to witness the transaction. If there were 9 people there and 7 came, how many would have been there?

If there were fifteen and seven left, how many would be there?

If there were 80 and 40 more came, how many would be in attendance?

If there were 130 and 60 left, how many would remain?

Let's say there are 140. What if 80 left? How many would still be there?

Now, figure out how many would still be there if these left: 10, 4, 7, and 13.

If there were 100 people and 3 left, how many would be remaining?

How many people would still be there if 30 left, or 37, or 74?

What if there were 248 people there and five times more came. How many people would be there?

Day 92

$23/100 = 23\%$ % is the percent sign

$37/100 =$ $14/100 =$

$6/100 =$ $75/100 =$

How many cents are in one dollar?

What percent of a dollar is one penny?

What percent of a dollar is one nickel?

What percent of a dollar is one dime?

What percent of a dollar is one quarter?

Write the fraction, the percent, and the money amount in dollars for each of the coin amounts above. Do it for one dollar as well.

Day 93

Write down ten. Can you draw a decimal point to turn it into a 1?

Now figure out how much money you would earn from your investment of twenty dollars, fifty dollars, and eighty dollars.

Now let's invest at just 1 percent. Write the number ten again. Can you draw in a decimal point to make it say ten cents?

Write the number ten one more time. This time place a decimal point but make it say ten dollars.

Write $10.00 x 10 = $100.00 and watch what happens to the decimal point.

A percent is a part of a whole, like a fraction.

What's ten percent of $100? $10
What's ten percent of $10? $1
What's ten percent of $1 $0.10
What's ten percent of $0.10 $0.01

Figure out how much money you would have after your investment of seven dollars and two hundred dollars. Figure out the total amount of money you would have after you earned ten percent on your investment and then again with earning one percent on your investment.

7 dollars at 10% =   7 dollars at 1% =

200 dollars at 10% =   200 dollars at 1% =

Now find the difference between what you earned at ten and one percent.

Day 94

$$75,975$$
$$-\ 51,348$$

$$390,468$$
$$-\ 128,128$$

How many legs do six chickens and nine cats have?

34,526 x 5 =

34,526 x 10 =

34,526 x 50 =

34,526 x 100 =

34,526 x 500 =

34,526 x 1000 =

34,526 x 5000 =

34,526 x 5555 =

How would you figure out what's 34,526 x 6666? (Think! Don't multiply.)

Day 95
Review

If there were 100 people and 13 left, how many would still be there?

How many people would still be there if 78 went home?

What if there were 537 people there when Abraham bought the field and five times more came. How many people would have wound up watching?

Write the fraction, the percent, and the money amount in dollars for each of these amounts: three cents, twelve cents, one dollar.

Write equations to find the sum and difference of three and twelve cents.

You can divide 15 and 100 each by 5 to find an equivalent fraction.

7,819 x 6 =

Day 96
Review

```
   37          $1.00          37
  567        - $0.47        x  58
+ 270        -------       -------
-------
```

$3/8 + 4/8 =$

$3\ 2/3 - 1\ 1/3 =$

$7.20 x 4 =

Find 60 percent of this number. (50% = 0.50, 145 x 0.50 = 50% of 145)

145

Write seven and two tenths as a decimal and fraction.

Day 97
Review

478	$1.00	79
+ 362	- $0.62	x 56

Write these numbers as decimals and then convert them to mixed numbers: fourteen and seven tenths as well as three and nine tenths.

Compare these numbers and draw a greater than and less than symbol between the sets of numbers.

7.6   8.5   11   10.9

Day 98
Review

Write these numbers and then read them out loud.

<u>hundred</u> thousand | <u>ten</u> thousand | <u>one</u> thousand , <u>hundreds</u> | <u>tens</u> | <u>ones</u>

twenty-three thousand, six hundred seven

Draw a polygon.   Find the difference. 251 - 74

Multiply.
        34 x 51 =

        29 x 87 =

Day 99
Review

Let's say you had fifty-two dollars of debt and got in five hundred twenty-six dollars. How much money would you have after you paid your debt?

Add together three and one third and fifteen and one third.

$$
\begin{array}{r}
700 \\
- 241 \\
\hline
\end{array}
$$

42 x 38 =

Day 100
Review

What's $1.00 - $0.70?

What's $1.00 - $0.73?

Subtract. Then add to check to see if your answers make sense!

$1.00	$1.00	$1.00
-$0.51	-$0.18	-$0.87

Add these amounts: seventeen dollars and sixty-five cents, fourteen dollars and forty cents, twenty-six dollars and seventy cents, forty-six dollars and fifteen cents, one hundred five dollars and sixteen cents.

Day 101
Review

870 x 13 =

290 x 57 =

Do the opposite to check my work.   2536 ÷ 8 = 317

Day 102
Review

Find your profit. Buy at $13.72, and sell at $74.59.

If the altar weighed eight times as much as the ram on it and the ram was 137 pounds, how much did the altar weigh?

If the altar weighs forty-seven times the weight of the wood piled on it, how much does it weigh if the wood is twenty-three ounces.

Day 103
Review

If the altar weighs 37 times the weight of the ram on it, and the ram is 460 ounces, how much does the altar weigh?

520 x 78 =

What's 3600 grams in kilograms?

What's 2.5 kilograms in grams?

Draw a line that is 4.25 inches long.

Day 104
Review

If there were 100 people there to witness the transaction of Abraham buying the field and 13 left, how many would be remaining?

How many people would remain if 78 left from 100?

If there were 537 people to witness Abraham buying the field and five times more came, how many more people would be there? How many would there be all together?

Day 105
Review

Write the fraction of a dollar, the percent of a dollar, and the money amount in dollars for each of these amounts: seventeen cents and three dollars.

Write equations to find the sum and difference of three dollars and twelve cents and twelve dollars and twenty-five cents.

627 x 9 =

Day 106

Draw a circle to be the flock all together. Divide it into four parts. Color in three parts. Let's say that part of the flock had been watered. What part of the flock is still thirsty?

Write the fraction that shows what part of the flock had gotten a drink.

Which is bigger? Use < or > to show it.

How much of the flock is represented by those who have had a drink and those who haven't?

Draw seven circles. Let's say those represent seven sheep before Jacob watered them. How many had a drink so far?

What fractions could you add together to get to one?

Let's start with the whole flock and subtract off those who have had their drink. How many haven't if two fifths have?

What about if five sixths have?

What about if five twelfths have?

What about if seven ninths have?

Day 107

 What time is it?

I'm going to tell you two times. One is when Leah was snuck into Jacob's tent. One is when he found out he had been tricked. You are going to draw the times on the clocks and then figure out how much time has elapsed, how long it took them to get there.

Leah snuck in at ten at night and Jacob found out at five in the afternoon.

Try it with these times: 11:00 AM and 3:00 PM.

Elapsed time: Elapsed time:

Count by fives to figure out how many minutes that is.

What time does the first clock say?

What time is it on the second clock?

Now draw these times and figure how long it took Jacob to learn he had been tricked. Leah snuck into his tent at ten thirty at night and Jacob found out at six in the morning.

Find the elapsed time with these times: 12:15 PM and 3:30 PM.

Elapsed time: Elapsed time:

Draw these times and figure how long it took Jacob to figure out he had been tricked.

seven twenty at night and four forty-five that following morning

9:05 AM and 3:27 PM

Elapsed time: Elapsed time:

Day 108

What's three four times?   What's three times six?

Count by fives with tally marks to figure out five times five and five times seven.

Use tally marks to ten to figure out what is one half times ten.

What's one half times eight?   What's one half times twelve?

Multiplying by ½ is the same as dividing by two or finding half the number. So, what's 20 times ½?

10 x 1 =   10 x 0 =   10 x 10 =

340 x 25 =

570 x 42 =

680 x 91 =

Day 109

If two sons were born and one was born to Leah, what fraction of the sons were born to Leah? Draw two people. Circle one of them. Write the fraction showing how many were Leah's sons.

Add three more people to your drawing. They all represent Jacob's sons. Circle two of them to show that two were Leah's sons. How do you think you would show the fraction of how many of the boys were Leah's sons?

Add two more sons to your drawing and circle two more. Write the new fraction.

If three fifths were Leah's sons and then two fifths were her maid's sons, how many of the sons were "from" Leah? Draw a picture to show three fifths. Draw five sons and circle three of them. Then circle two more. Write the equation with the answer.

Write another fractional equation that equals one.

If Jacob had seven sons and three were Leah's, write an equation with the answer to show what fraction of the group that were not hers.

Write another fraction subtraction equation.

Day 110
Review

How much of the flock hasn't had a drink yet if three fifths have? What about if four ninths have?

Draw these times and figure how long it took Jacob to realize he had been tricked.

seven ten at night and two fifty in the morning
8:25 PM and 3:57 AM

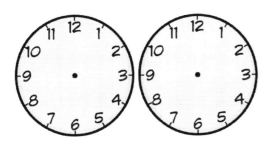 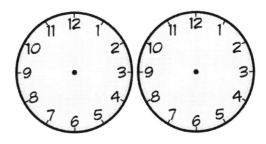

Elapsed time: Elapsed time:

370 x 28 =

Day 111

If the servant was given five talents and returned with double, how many talents did he have in the end?

If the servant was given twelve talents and came back with double, how many talents did he have in the end?

If the servant was given forty-three talents and got back double, how many talents did he have in the end?

Let's say the servant was given eight talents and, in the end, just had five when he returned. What happened?

8 talents _____ = 5 talents

If the servant ended up with twenty-four talents and had started with seven, how many talents did he earn along the way?

If the servant ended up with one hundred thirteen talents and had started with seventy-six, how many talents did he earn?

If the servant ended up with two hundred twenty-two talents and had started with one hundred five, how many talents did he earn?

If the servant started with ten talents and ended with four talents, how many talents did he "earn?"

If the servant earned five times the amount he was given, how much did he earn if he had been given 27 talents?

If the servant earned twenty-four times the amount he was given, how much did he earn if he had been given 39 talents?

If the servant earned eight times the amount he was given, how much did he earn if he had been given 356 talents?

If the servant started with one hundred talents and ended with forty-six talents, how many talents did he "earn?"

Day 112

One liter is 1000 milliliters. How many milliliters is two liters of oil?

How many liters of oil is 5000 milliliters of oil?

How many milliliters is half a liter?

Cut out the pieces in your workbook and figure out the following:

How many cups are in a pint?

How many pints are in one quart?

How many quarts are in a gallon?

Use what you know. How many pints are in a gallon?

How many cups are in a quart?

How many cups are in a gallon?

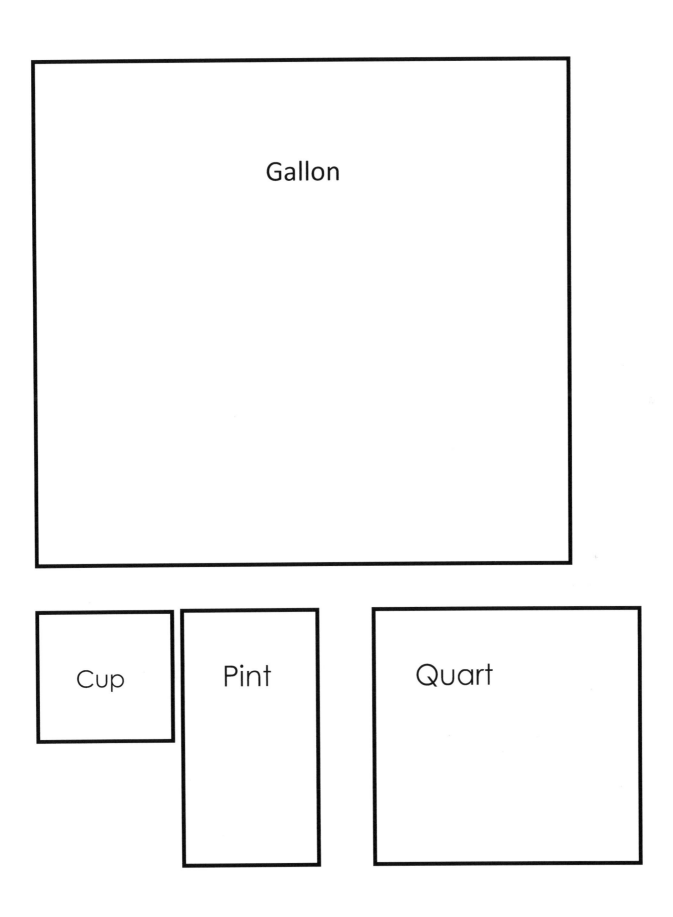

Gallon

Cup

Pint

Quart

Day 113

The capital letter I represents the number 1. What number do you think is III?

The capital letter V represents the number 5. What number do you think is VI?

The capital letter X represents the number 10. What number do you think is XV?

Figure out what these numbers are:

VII =   XVI =   II =   XIII =

If VI is 6, what do you think is IV?

XVI is ten, five, one or sixteen. What's XIV?

Figure out these numbers:

XX =   IX =   XIX =   XIV =

Let's learn more letters. L = 50 and C = 100 What would be XL?

How would you write 300?

How would you write:

150 =   190 =

340 =   280 =

Day 114

We're going to read and write Roman Numerals today again. Do you remember how to write 1, 5, or 10?

How do you think you would write 15?

Figure out what these numbers are:

VIII =   XX =   XVII =   XI =

XI is eleven. What's IX?

Figure out these numbers:

IX =   XXIV =   XIII =   XXXVI =

Do you remember what letters represent 50 and 100?

How would you write 253?

How would you write:

175 =

196 =

284 =

Day 115
Review

There are 8 pints in a gallon. There are 4 cups in a quart. How many cups are in a gallon?

If the servant earned six times what he had been given, how much did he earn if he had been given 297 talents?

If the servant started with one hundred talents and ended with thirty-one talents, how many talents did he "earn?"

How would you write 93, 394, and 178 in Roman numerals?

93 =

394 =

178 =

Day 116

Write an amount of money with a bunch of zeros. Make sure to use a dollar sign and decimal point.

Now double that amount.   Now double that amount.   Now double that amount.

Here's a subtraction example.

	$3.15	315
	- $1.20	- 120
	2.00	200
	-.10	-10
	+.05	5
	$1.95	195 -> $1.95

Let's say the tunic is usually priced $42.95, but today it's on sale for just $15.80. How much could you save if you bought it today?

You buy the tunic for $42.95 and thread for $3.76. How much did you spend?

Let's say the tunic is usually priced $62.05, but today it's on sale for just $23.80. How much could you save if you bought it today?

You buy the tunic for $78.50 and a yarn for $4.67. How much did you spend?

Let's say the tunic is ten times more expensive than the cloak that costs $35.17. How much does the tunic cost?

What do you think is $35.17 times ten if 3517 times ten is 35,170?

Now multiply $35.17 by 100. First think, what's 3517 times 100?

Multiply these amounts by ten and one hundred:

$2.05

$14.67

$243.99

Day 117

You are going to draw a map. Mark one place on the page, "You are here." Mark another place on the page as where the brothers and flock were.

Draw streets to get from here to there.

Decide how far each centimeter or inch on your drawing is in miles or kilometers.

Measure the distance along the roads Joseph would need to travel to get to the brothers and the flock.

Multiply that amount by the distance represented by each measurement.

How far would Joseph need to travel to get there?

Day 118

If you sold six bags of cookies to each of three customers, how many bags of cookies did you sell all together?

What if you sold three bags of cookies to each of six customers, how many bags would you have sold all together?

What if you received two votes from three different families for best snowman, how many votes did you receive all together?

How many votes did you receive if you received 3 votes from two different families?

If you sold twelve bags of cookies to each of three customers, how many bags of cookies did you sell all together?

What if you sold three bags of cookies to each of twelve customers, how many bags would you have sold all together?

What if you received twenty-one votes from three different families for best snowman, how many votes did you receive all together?

How many votes did you receive if you received 3 votes from twenty-one different families?

If you sold twelve bags of cookies in total to three people, how many bags of cookies did you sell to each person if they each bought the same number of bags?

If you sold twenty bags of cookies in total to four people, how many bags of cookies did you sell to each person if they each bought the same number of bags?

Let's say you got forty votes from ten families. Divide to find out about how many people voted from each family.

If you sold sixty-four bags of cookies to each of three customers, how many bags of cookies did you sell all together?

What if you received twenty-seven votes from three different families for best snowman, how many votes did you receive all together?

If you sold three bags of cookies to each of one hundred fifty-eight customers, how many bags of cookies did you sell?

What if you received three votes from two hundred thirty-six voters for best snowman (for most creative, best design, highest quality construction), how many votes did you receive?

Day 119

Now draw these times and figure how long Joseph was in the pit. They threw him in at ten in the morning and got him out at ten thirty. They threw him in at 11:00 PM and got him out at 11:30 PM.

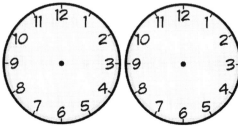 

Elapsed time: _____   Elapsed time: _____

They threw him in at nine in the morning and got him out at ten thirty-five.
Then let's say they threw him in at 11:15 AM and got him out at 11:40 AM.

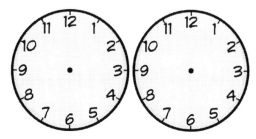

Elapsed time: _____   Elapsed time: _____

They threw him in at eight twenty at night and got him out at ten forty. Then let's say they threw him in at 10:55 AM and pulled him out at 11:25 AM.

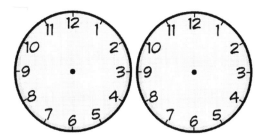 

Elapsed time: _____   Elapsed time: _____

Day 120
Review

Let's say the tunic is ten times more expensive than the cloak that costs $28.97. How much does the tunic cost?

If the tunic cost 100 times the cost of the cloth at $1.23, how much does the tunic cost?

Draw a line that's eight centimeters long and write how far that would be if that distance were on a map where each centimeter represented 150 miles.

If you sold seven bags of cookies to each of two hundred thirty-nine customers, how many bags of cookies did you sell?

Draw these times and figure how long Joseph was in the pit. They threw him in at 9:35 AM and got him out at 11:10.

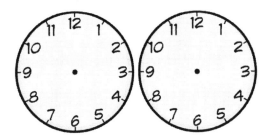

Elapsed time:

Day 121

If the house were five yards long and ten yards wide, what would its area be?

What would you need to know to find the surface area of the whole room, the total area of all the surfaces you want to paint?

Let's say there was a room that was the shape of a perfect cube. What would that look like? How many sides would it have?

In a perfect cube each of the six sides is a square. If each side had an area of 5 meters squared, what would be the total surface area of the cube?

Find the surface area of a cube where each side is a square with a length of ten centimeters.

What would be the surface area of a cube where each side had a length of five inches?

What would be the surface area of a cube where each side had a length of twenty-three centimeters?

What would be the surface area of a cube where each side had a length of eighteen inches?

What would be the surface area of a cube where each side had a length of twenty-five centimeters?

Day 122

Roll a die over and over again and jot down a tally mark in each column when that number comes up. Do it about thirty times.

Did one number come up more than the others?

Is it more likely that one number would come up compared to another number?

If you rolled the die right now one time, is it likely or unlikely that you'll roll a two?

Would it be likely or unlikely that you didn't roll a two?

Flip a coin twenty times. Record what side it lands on each time. What is the outcome? What should be the outcome?

What's the chance of a head coming up? You can write that as a fraction. $1/2$

If there was one red, one blue, and one yellow marble in a bowl, and you picked one out, what are the chances you picked out the blue one?

Day 123

If you were given $100 three times, how much would you have?

What if you were given $120 dollars three times?

What if you were given $123 dollars three times?

If you were given $1000 three times, how much would you have?

If you were given $1400 three times, how much would you have?

If you were given $1430 three times, how much would you have?

If you were given $1436 three times, how much would you have?

If you were given $674 three times, how much would you have?

If you were given $49 thirty-three times, how much would you have?

Day 124

If one piece of silver was worth $4.23, how much would two pieces be worth?

$4.23
+ $4.23

If one piece of silver was worth $32.14, how much would two pieces be worth?

$32.14
+ $32.14

If one piece of silver was worth $0.50, how much would two pieces be worth?

If one piece of silver was worth $1.50, how much would two pieces be worth?

If one piece of silver was worth $10.50, how much would two pieces be worth?

If one piece of silver was worth $6.47, how much would two pieces be worth?

$6.47
+ $6.47

If one piece of silver was worth $23.61, how much would two pieces be worth?

$23.61
+ $23.61

If one piece of silver was worth $40.75, how much would two pieces be worth?

$40.75
+ $40.75

If one piece of silver was worth $46.99, how much would two pieces be worth?

$$\begin{array}{r} \$46.99 \\ + \$46.99 \\ \hline \end{array}$$

If one piece of silver was worth $128.27, how much would two pieces be worth?

$$\begin{array}{r} \$128.27 \\ + \$128.27 \\ \hline \end{array}$$

If one piece of silver was worth $135.90, how much would two pieces be worth?

$$\begin{array}{r} \$135.90 \\ + \$135.90 \\ \hline \end{array}$$

If one piece of silver was worth $281.50, how much would two pieces be worth?

$$\begin{array}{r} \$281.50 \\ + \$281.50 \\ \hline \end{array}$$

Day 125
Review

What would be the surface area of a cube where each side had a length of thirty-eight inches?

What's the chance of a tail coming up when you flip a coin? (Write it as a fraction.)

If there was one red, one blue, and one yellow marble in a bowl, and you picked one out, what are the chances you picked out the red one?

If you were given $498 three times, how much would you have?

If one piece of silver was worth $367.81, how much would two pieces be worth?

$367.81
+ $367.81

Day 126

Write one third and two thirds as fractions.

If there had been ten baskets and the birds had eaten out of half of them, how many would that be?

Draw ten baskets. Probably best to just draw ten circles. Put an X in three of them and write the fraction and decimal shown by the picture. Put an X in one more and write that fraction. Do the same thing two more times.

Draw a box and divide into four parts.

Add together the four fractions you wrote in the previous section.

What mixed number does eighteen tenths equal?

Each of the fractions below is an equivalent fraction to either three tenths, four tenths, five tenths, or six tenths. An equivalent fraction is an equal fraction, like $1/2 = 2/4$. You can draw a picture of a box and divide into four parts and then color in half of it to show that it is true. Write the equivalent fraction of each of these fractions.

$6/20 =$ $\qquad$ $3/5 =$ $\qquad$ $1/2 =$ $\qquad$ $9/30 =$

Bonus: Reduce eight tenths. Make the numerator and denominator smaller.

Day 127

Write one ninth as a fraction.

If two fifths of the dream was about the cows and then three fifths of the dream was about the ears of grain, how much of the dream would that have been?

If the cow part of the dream was two sevenths of it and then the grain part was four sevenths of the dream, how much of the dream was that?

If the cow part of the dream was one ninth of the dream and then the ear part was four ninths of the dream, how much of the dream was that?

Try it with three eighths and four eighths.

Write the equation and answer with mixed numbers. If three and two thirds of his dreams were about the cows and ears and one and one third was about the ears of grain, how much of his dreams were about the cows?

Try it with fourteen and three fifths with eight and one fifth.

Try it with thirty and seven ninths with sixteen and two ninths.

Try it with twelve fifths and six fifths. Write the equation and answer with improper fractions (where the numerator is bigger than the denominator) and then again with mixed numbers.

Day 128

Draw a picture that shows one half.

Write out those fifths you just answered, from one fifth to five fifths.

Add together the fractions you just wrote.

If you had fifteen fingers, how many hands would you have?

Draw five circles. Color in one of them. Color in half of each of the other circles. Add together the colored parts. How much do you have? Write the equation and the answer. 1 + ½ + ... =

If you had four and a half circles colored in and then erased one and a half of them, how many would be colored in?

Subtract forty and seven eighths minus twelve and three eighths.

Day 129

What fraction describes one of the two pieces of Egypt if it were divided in half?

Draw a picture that shows six out of seven things, six sevenths, 6/7 .

Draw a picture that shows three out of four parts of one whole object, three fourths, $3/4$.

Add one and one fourth plus three and two fourths.

Add twenty-five and one fifth plus seventeen and three fifths.

If Egypt were divided in two, and one part was $1/8$ of the whole land, what fraction shows the size of the other part?

If Egypt was in two parts, and one part was $3/14$ of the whole of Egypt, what fraction shows the size of the other part?

Find the difference between one hundred and seven fifteenths and thirty-four and two fifteenths.

Find the difference between fifty-two and eight fifteenths and seven and three fifteenths.

Find the sum of seven twelfths and eight twelfths. Write your answer as an improper fraction and then as a mixed number. Then reduce the fractional part of the mixed number.

Day 130
Review

What mixed number does seventeen tenths equal? Remember that a mixed number is a whole number and a fraction together.

Can you fill in the blank in the equivalent fraction?

$^8/_{40} = {^?}/_{10}$ $^1/_2 = {^?}/_{24}$ $^1/_5 = {^?}/_{25}$

If fourteen fifths of Pharaoh's dreams were about cows and ears of grain and two fifths of the dreams were about the cows, how much of his dreams were about ears of grain? Write the equation and answer with improper fractions (where the numerator is bigger than the denominator) and then write the answer as a mixed number.

Subtract thirty and four eighths minus twenty-four and one eighth.

Find the sum of seven fifteenths and eleven fifteenths. Write your answer as an improper fraction and then as a mixed number. Then reduce the fractional part of the mixed number.

Day 131

How many cities had Joseph not reached yet if he's reached two fifths so far?

Draw these times and figure how long it took them to reach the mountains. They started at seven ten in the morning and got there at two forty-eight that afternoon. Try it with: 8:25 AM and got there at 2:28 PM.

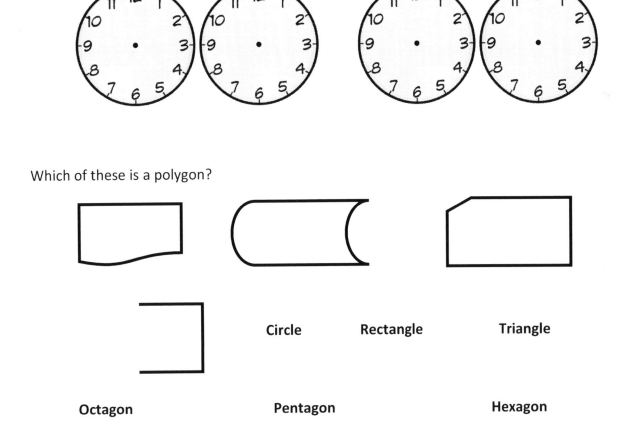

Which of these is a polygon?

Circle   Rectangle   Triangle

Octagon   Pentagon   Hexagon

Day 132

There are 4 quarts in a gallon. There are 2 cups in a pint. There are 2 pints in a quart.

How many cups are in two gallons? (Draw a picture if that helps.)

How would you write 39 and 258 in Roman Numeral?

```
   295          $1.00          64
 + 676        - $0.76        x 39
```

Day 133

Let's say the tunic is ten times more expensive than the watch that costs $15.98. How much does the tunic cost?

If the tunic cost 100 times the cost of the cloth at $4.57, how much does the tunic cost?

478	478	$1.00	79
+ 362	- 199	- $0.62	x 56

Day 134

What would be the surface area of a cube where each side had a length of sixty-seven inches?

What's the chance of a tail coming up when you flip a coin? (Write it as a fraction.)

If there was one red, one blue, and one yellow marble in a bowl, and you picked one out, what are the chances you picked out the red one?

607	417	$1.00	48
+ 554	- 278	- $0.39	x 2000

Day 135

If you were given $576 three times, how much would you have?

If one piece of silver was worth $249.56, how much would two piece be worth?

If you sold seven bags of cookies to each of two hundred thirty-nine customers, how many bags of cookies did you sell?

527
+ 765

653
- 287

$1.00
- $0.46

Day 136

If the slave earned seven times the amount of the original investment, how much did she earn if she had been given 369 talents?

If a slave started with one hundred talents and ended with thirty-one talents, how many talents did he "earn?"

Figure out how much money you would have after your investment of eight dollars and seven hundred dollars. Figure out the total amount of money you would have after you earned ten percent and one percent on your investment. (Hint: How would you write seven cents and 100 cents? 0.07 and 1.00.)

$$
\begin{array}{r}
755 \\
+\ 362 \\
\hline
\end{array}
\qquad
\begin{array}{r}
325 \\
-\ 127 \\
\hline
\end{array}
\qquad
\begin{array}{r}
\$1.00 \\
-\ \$0.41 \\
\hline
\end{array}
$$

Day 137

Draw a line that is eight centimeters long. How far would that be if on a map each centimeter represented 270 miles?

Draw these times and figure out how much time elapsed. 8:42 PM and 10:20 AM

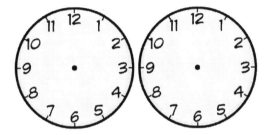

577	315	$1.00	34
+ 509	- 132	- $0.12	x 77

Day 138

What mixed number does nineteen tenths equal? Remember that a mixed number is a whole number and a fraction together.

Can you fill in the blank in the equivalent fraction?

$$^4/_{20} = ^?/_{10}$$ $$^1/_2 = ^?/_{12}$$

If thirteen fifths of Pharaoh's dreams were about cows and grain and two fifths were about cows, how much of his dreaming was about grain? Write the equation and answer with improper fractions (where the numerator is bigger than the denominator) and then again with a mixed number.

$$\begin{array}{r} 938 \\ + 162 \\ \hline \end{array} \qquad \begin{array}{r} 625 \\ - 436 \\ \hline \end{array} \qquad \begin{array}{r} \$1.00 \\ - \$0.74 \\ \hline \end{array} \qquad \begin{array}{r} 34 \\ \times 81 \\ \hline \end{array}$$

Day 139

Subtract thirty-four and five eighths minus twenty-three and two eighths.

Find the sum of fourteen fifteenths and eleven fifteenths. Write your answer as an improper fraction and then as a mixed number. Then reduce the fractional part of the mixed number.

```
   2900          1100          5000
 + 5800         - 810         x  31
```

Day 140

If you were given $395 three times, how much would you have?

If one piece of silver was worth $283.74, how much would two piece be worth?

If you sold eight bags of cookies to each of two hundred forty-nine customers, how many bags of cookies did you sell?

$$
\begin{array}{r}
695 \\
+ 732 \\
\hline
\end{array}
\qquad
\begin{array}{r}
490 \\
- 436 \\
\hline
\end{array}
\qquad
\begin{array}{r}
\$1.00 \\
- \$0.27 \\
\hline
\end{array}
$$

Day 141

1965	5028	4527	910
+ 2087	+ 2569	+ 2653	+ 190

What's four times seven hundred and fourteen?

Find the sum: 35 + 67 + 123 =

Multiply:

4 x 6 =   5 x 3 =   6 x 3 =   3 x 8 =

7 x 6 =   7 x 7 =   9 x 9 =   8 x 8 =

5 x 6 =   7 x 3 =   8 x 4 =   9 x 8 =

Day 142

2704	3591	158	5674
+ 1808	+ 4520	+ 27	+ 183

How many pieces of fruit were gathered all together if 173 apples, 26 oranges, and 54 pears were gathered?

What is thirty times six?

What is sixty-eight times eight?

What is eighty-seven times seven?

Day 143

1529	3705	2983	569
+ 465	+ 2738	+ 6043	+ 257

If there had been 51 people in attendance and 7 left, how many would still be there?

If you owed $18 dollars and paid $6 a day, how long would it take you to pay off your debt?

Double these numbers.

75   49   150

Day 144

3098	1657	2758	560
+ 2835	+ 3329	+ 6534	+ 173

How many cards would you have received if you received eight cards nine times?

Write one thousand six hundred twenty-seven on the place value chart.

thousand	hundreds	tens	ones

Write four thousand one hundred seven in expanded form.

What is this number in standard form (just as a normal number)?

7000 + 500 + 8

Day 145

```
  445        568        458        329
+ 176      + 254      + 287      +  95
```

```
  2217       2044       176        473
+ 2839     + 4956     + 378      + 59
```

```
  70         63         82         76
x  9       x  6       x  3       x  4
```

70 + 70 + 70 + 70 + 70 + 70 =

$$
\begin{array}{r}
273 \\
-\ 95 \\
\hline
\end{array}
\qquad
\begin{array}{r}
754 \\
-\ 278 \\
\hline
\end{array}
\qquad
\begin{array}{r}
355 \\
-\ 36 \\
\hline
\end{array}
\qquad
\begin{array}{r}
246 \\
-\ 174 \\
\hline
\end{array}
$$

346 + 257 =

17 x 3 =   46 x 9 =

19 x 3 =   78 x 5 =

Day 147

372   654   562   496
- 145   - 289   - 75   - 78

Read this clock.

What would be the area of a rectangle that is eight blocks in a row with six rows?

Day 148

```
  634        232        753        532
- 235      - 195      -  67      - 182
```

Draw a shape and color in three-fourths of it. Write three-fourths.

How many dollars would you need to get to three hundred seventy-four dollars if you had thirty-eight dollars of debt?

17 x 4 =   96 x 8 =

Day 149

```
  305        1580        4632         564
-  49       -  791       -  783       - 182
```

How many lines of symmetry does a triangle have?

Find the difference between 621 miles and 175 miles.

27 x 4 =   53 x 8 =

```
   472        1542       1637        134
 - 163       - 784      -  858      -  56
```

```
  2304        8422        425        159
 -  444      -  756      -  89      -  87
```

$100 - 40 =$

$140 - 50 =$

$371 \times 4 =$ $367 \times 7 =$

Day 151

Find the perimeter of these shapes by using multiplication. Let's say all the measurements are centimeters.

 439

Find the area of a rectangle that's 58 inches wide and 74 inches long.

On the protractor draw a line from zero to the center. Then draw lines to 30° and 130°.

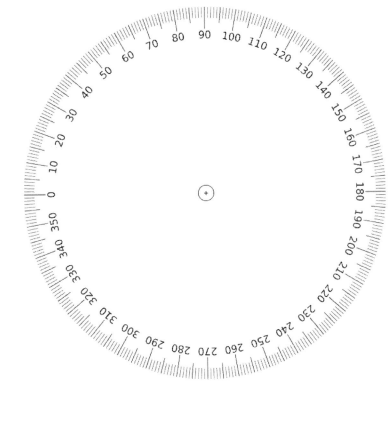

Day 152

```
    45              94          (You could just multiply 38 x 6 and
  x 76            x 38            subtract that from 3800. Why?)
```

How many minutes are in thirty-nine hours?

Let's say that Laban and Isaac had together six hundred forty-two sheep. Isaac had one hundred twenty-one sheep, and of those, ninety-five had wool that wasn't all white. How many of Isaac's sheep were all white?

Day 153

$$
\begin{array}{r}
827 \\
95 \\
+\ 345 \\
\hline
\end{array}
\qquad
\begin{array}{r}
1600 \\
-\ 700 \\
\hline
\end{array}
\qquad
\begin{array}{r}
248 \\
\times\ 5 \\
\hline
\end{array}
\qquad
\begin{array}{r}
100 \\
-\ 28 \\
\hline
\end{array}
$$

What's the value of eight nickels, ten quarters, twelve dimes, and seven pennies?

Let's say that Egypt had been divided into fifteen sectors for Joseph to visit to set up his plan for the time of abundance. Let's say that at this point, Joseph has visited six of the areas. Write as fractions the part of Egypt visited and unvisited so far. Then use the > greater than sign or the < less than sign to show which fraction is greater. (The big end of the sign should point to the bigger number, and the small end of the sign should point to the smaller number.)

Day 154

```
  567          100           48         1000
   91         - 17         x 94         - 620
+ 248
```

Let's say that an orchard had 9 trees and each tree had 237 pieces of fruit on it. How many pieces of fruit are there all together?

Round these numbers to the nearest hundred.

249 →   350 →   719→   651→

Write an addition equation and a subtraction equation that give the answer $9/16$.

Day 155

```
   823          5000          291          500
    75        -  800        x  70        -  37
 + 764
```

```
   823          1100          241          100
    95        -  400          175        -  58
 + 325                      + 430
```

```
   317           145            89
 x   5         x   6         x  46
```

Day 156

986	$1.00	185	$1.00
+ 75	- $0.40	x 30	- $0.48

Let's say Abraham went 89 miles in one day and 42 of the miles were traveled after lunch. <u>About</u> how far did he travel before lunch?

Let's say Abraham stayed 184 days in each of 7 towns. How many days did He stay all together?

Do it three ways. First, estimate by rounding the number of days to the nearest hundred and multiply by 7. Then estimate by rounding both the number of days and the number of towns to the nearest ten and multiply to find the answer. Then solve the exact answer. Which was the best estimate?

Day 157

```
   486          $1.00          964          $1.00
 + 187        - $0.30        +  87        - $0.36
```

Compare these numbers using a greater than/less than symbol.

27,011   26,978   8 rows of 347 plants   5 rows of 498 plants

Let's say Abraham arrived at 9:13 in the morning and stayed until 2:25 in the afternoon. How long was he on the mountain? Draw the times and then figure out the elapsed time.

Elapsed time:

Day 158

600	$11.00	38	$1.00
85	- $4.00	x 57	- $0.71
+ 315			

Combine these numbers. 253, - 75, 72, - 152, 187, - 79

How many pieces of fruit are in an orchard if there are 800 trees and each tree has 40 pieces of fruit?

Find what number fits in these blanks.

_____ - 59 = 154   164 + _____ = 620

Day 159

How much would seven trains cost if one train was 89 cents?

```
   723          $1.00          47          $1.00
    97        - $0.60        x 86        - $0.38
 + 255
```

Draw a hexagon and write its coordinates.

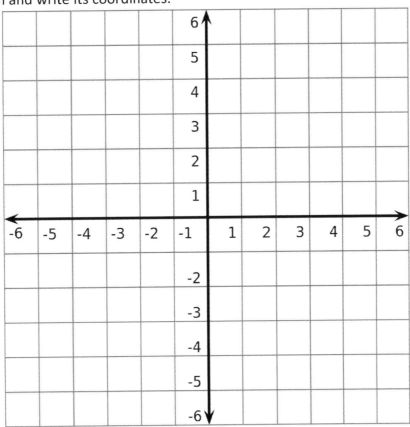

By H Padleckas via Wikimedia Commons

Day 160

```
   271          1500          97         $1.00
    48         - 800         607       - $0.29
 + 469                     + 322
```

```
   123          1400         441         $1.00
    58         - 500         105       - $0.17
 + 194                     + 538
```

```
   428           56          386
 x   5         x 76        x  40
```

Day 161

37	$1.00	37
567	- $0.47	x 58
+ 270		

How would you write 79 and 241 in Roman Numerals?

Measure two things in your house and write down their measurement in centimeters. Use a decimal.

Write twelve and seven tenths as a decimal and fraction.

Day 162

478	$1.00	79
+ 362	- $0.62	x 56

Write these numbers as decimals and then convert them to fractions: four and three tenths as well as twenty-one and five tenths.

Compare these numbers and draw a greater than and less than symbol between the sets of numbers.

7.6   6.9   10.9   9.6

Day 163

Write these numbers and then read them out loud.

    <u>hundred</u> thousand | <u>ten</u> thousand | <u>one</u> thousand , <u>hundreds</u> | <u>tens</u> | <u>ones</u>

    seventeen thousand four

    two hundred thirty-five thousand seventy-one

Multiply.

    47 x 62 =

    35 x 76 =

Day 164

Let's say you had one hundred thirty-nine dollars of debt and got in five hundred twenty-six dollars. How much money would you have after you paid your debt?

Add together three and one third and fifteen and one third.

```
  700
- 241
```

49 x 62 =

Day 165

What's $1.00 - $0.30?

What's $1.00 - $0.37?

Find the difference. Then check to see if your answers make sense! Add the answer and what you subtracted together.

$$\begin{array}{r} \$1.00 \\ -\$0.51 \\ \hline \end{array} \qquad \begin{array}{r} \$1.00 \\ -\$0.18 \\ \hline \end{array} \qquad \begin{array}{r} \$1.00 \\ -\$0.87 \\ \hline \end{array}$$

Add these amounts: seven dollars and sixty-eight cents, fourteen dollars and forty-nine cents, twenty dollars and seventy-eight cents, sixty-five dollars and fifteen cents, one hundred thirty-five dollars and sixty-seven cents.

Day 166

63 x 570 =

39 x 820 =

Do the opposite to check my work.   2219 ÷ 7 = 316

Day 167

Find your profit. Buy at $24.99, and sell at $50.25.

If the altars weighed four times as much as the sacrifices on it and the sacrifices was 283 tons, how much did the altars weigh?

If the altar weighs fifty-six times the weight of sacrifice on it, how much does it weigh if the sacrifice is thirty-four ounces.

Day 168

If the altar weighs 29 times the weight of the sacrifice on it, and the sacrifice is 380 grams, how much does the altar weigh?

370 x 64 =

What's 4200 grams in kilograms?

What's 1.7 kilograms in grams?

Draw a line that is 8.2 inches long.

Day 169

If there were 100 people and 13 left, how many would still be there?

How many people out of 100 would still be there if 78 left?

What if there were 384 people watching Abraham making his agreement and six times more came. How many people were then there?

Day 170

Write the fraction of a dollar, the percent of a dollar, and the money amount in dollars for each of these amounts: twenty-eight cents and four dollars.

Write equations to find the sum and difference of five dollars and twelve cents and twenty dollars and thirty-seven cents.

584 x 9 =

Day 171

How many cities had Joseph not reached yet if he'd gotten to five sevenths so far?

Draw these times and figure how long it took them to reach the mountain. They started at seven fifty in the morning and got there at two forty-eight that afternoon. Try it also with: 8:25 AM and got there at 2:10 PM.

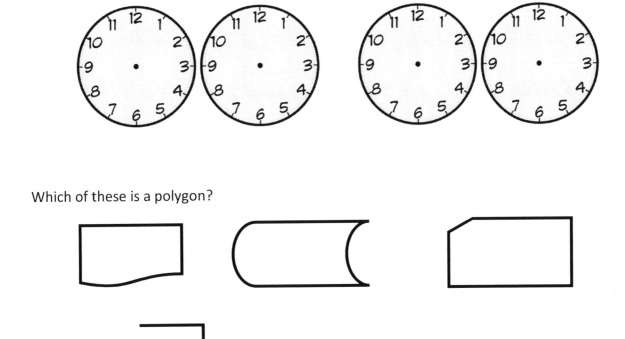

Which of these is a polygon?

Circle   Rectangle   Triangle

Octagon   Pentagon   Hexagon

Oval   Square

Day 172

There are 2 pints in a quart. There are 4 cups in a quart.

How many cups are in two quarts?

How would you write 89 and 244 in Roman Numeral?

$$185 + 673$$

$$\$1.00 - \$0.24$$

$$47 \times 58$$

Day 173

Let's say the watch is one hundred times more expensive than the tunic that costs $15.98. How much does the tunic cost?

If the tunic cost 10 times the cost of the cloth at $4.57, how much does the tunic cost?

$$457 + 297$$

$$705 - 238$$

$$\$1.00 - \$0.62$$

$$84 \times 39$$

Day 174

What would be the surface area of a cube where each side had a length of thirty-seven inches?

What's the chance of a tail coming up when you flip a coin? (Write it as a fraction.)

If there was one red, one blue, and one yellow marble in a bowl, and you picked one out, what are the chances you picked any color but red?

$$
\begin{array}{r} 567 \\ + 554 \\ \hline \end{array}
\qquad
\begin{array}{r} 417 \\ - 278 \\ \hline \end{array}
\qquad
\begin{array}{r} \$1.00 \\ - \$0.39 \\ \hline \end{array}
\qquad
\begin{array}{r} 37 \\ \times 29 \\ \hline \end{array}
$$

Day 175

If you were given $826 three times, how much would you have?

If one piece of silver was worth $324.56, how much would two piece be worth?

If you sold five bags of cookies to each of two hundred thirty-nine customers, how many bags of cookies did you sell?

482	546	$1.00
+ 765	- 157	- $0.46

Day 176

If the slave earned nine times the amount of the original investment, how much did she earn if she had been given 275 talents?

If a slave started with one hundred fifty talents and ended with sixty-one talents, how many talents did he "earn?"

Figure out how much money you would have after your investment of 9 dollars and three hundred dollars. Figure out the total amount of money you would have after you earned ten percent and one percent on your investment. (Hint: How would you write seven cents and 100 cents? 0.07 and 1.00.)

$$\begin{array}{r} 755 \\ + 486 \\ \hline \end{array}$$

$$\begin{array}{r} 804 \\ - 327 \\ \hline \end{array}$$

$$\begin{array}{r} \$1.00 \\ - \$0.41 \\ \hline \end{array}$$

Day 177

If you measured eight centimeters on a map, how far would that represent if each centimeter stood for 380 miles?

Draw these times and figure out how much time elapsed. 7:36 PM and 9:22 AM

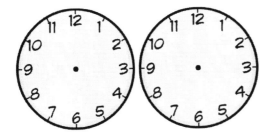

577	310	$1.00	47
+ 509	- 132	- $0.12	x 66

Day 178

What mixed number does thirteen tenths equal? Remember that a mixed number is a whole number and a fraction together.

Can you fill in the blank in the equivalent fraction?

$$^4/_{20} = {^?}/_{10}$$ $$^1/_2 = {^?}/_{12}$$

If eleven fifths of Pharaoh's dreams were about cows and grain and three fifths were about grain, how much of his dreaming was about cows? Write the equation and answer with improper fractions (where the numerator is bigger than the denominator) and then again with a mixed number.

$$\begin{array}{r} 845 \\ + 159 \\ \hline \end{array} \qquad \begin{array}{r} 511 \\ - 436 \\ \hline \end{array} \qquad \begin{array}{r} \$1.00 \\ - \$0.74 \\ \hline \end{array} \qquad \begin{array}{r} 54 \\ \times 91 \\ \hline \end{array}$$

Day 179

Subtract thirty-one and three sevenths minus twenty-three and two sevenths.

Find the sum of seven sixteenths and twelve sixteenths. Write your answer as an improper fraction and then as a mixed number.

636	515	$1.00	24
+ 154	- 236	- $0.74	x 76

Day 180

If you were given $289 three times, how much would you have?

If one piece of silver was worth $392.68, how much would two piece be worth?

If you sold nine bags of cookies to each of one hundred thirty-four customers, how many bags of cookies did you sell?

786	890	$1.00
+ 738	- 436	- $0.27

Thank you for using the Genesis Curriculum.
Hope you had a great year of learning together.

Look for more years of the Genesis Curriculum using both Old and New Testament books of the Bible. Find us online at genesiscurriculum.com to read about the latest developments in this expanding curriculum.

GC Steps are three years of preschool and kindergarten that prepare students in reading, writing, and math. These are aimed at children ages three to six.

Facts practice workbooks allow students to improve on their score each day using the same timed practice sheet daily.

The Genesis Curriculum Rainbow Readers take quality reading and present them in a new way. Each book stands alone and has a dictionary with the included vocabulary underlined in the text. The books have also been edited to use modern American spelling to help your children spell by knowing what looks right. Some of the books have been lightly edited for content issues. There are also occasional helps with explanations or pictures. They were made with GC students in mind.

GenesisCurriculum.com

Made in the USA
Columbia, SC
09 May 2022

60182147R00109